Voices of OKLAHOMA

STORIES FROM THE ORAL
HISTORY WEBSITE
Voices of Oklahoma.com

JOHN ERLING *with* JOHN HAMILL
and Oklahoma's Remarkable Storytellers

müllerhaus
[LEGACY]

TULSA

Voices of Oklahoma
John Erling with John Hamill

Müllerhaus Publishing Arts, Inc.
DBA Müllerhaus Legacy
5200 South Yale Ave, Penthouse | Tulsa, Oklahoma 74135
www.MullerhausLegacy.com

Printed in Canada.

ISBN-13: 978-0-9978410-9-1
LCCN: 2018960654

Cover Design by Laura Hyde
Interior Design by Laura Hyde

müllerhaus
[LEGACY]

THE CRAFT OF STORYTELLING. Great stories
surround us. Every family, organization, and community
is steeped in memories of triumph and loss, sacrifice
and love. But rarely are these stories woven together
in a way that captivates this generation and inspires
the next. That's where we can help. Whether on
printed page or in digital media, Müllerhaus Legacy guides you in preserving and
sharing your stories with a commitment that matches your passion. To be craftsmen
in the trade of storytelling, we've learned we must first be confidants in the art of
listening. Our uncompromising standards of personal care, professional service, and
attention to detail will make your experience with us its own magnificent adventure.
Your stories are your legacy. Telling your stories is ours. | **MullerhausLegacy.com**

ACKNOWLEDGMENTS

We gratefully acknowledge
Burt B. Holmes and the Chickasaw Nation
whose generous contributions made
this book possible.

Contents

Introduction

Voices on the radio have always intrigued me. As a young boy, I listened to *The Amos 'n Andy Show*, and *Fibber McGee and Molly*, hanging on to every syllable and wondering what those radio characters looked like. As I grew older, I was taken with the radio voices of personalities in the Midwest on Minneapolis and Chicago radio stations—and later in life, I was told that I myself had a radio voice. So, I have been voice-conscious for a long time.

I thought, *Wouldn't it be nice to listen to the voice of Thomas Jefferson? A rather high, thin voice, I am told.* And I became intrigued with the thought of oral histories—preserving the voices of today for future generations.

So, I became a voice collector. But with those voices came stories that sent me on a journey I could never have imagined. Oral history is recorded by pen or electronic devices. But it is the voice recording that brings you closer to the storyteller. It adds the extra dimension. Hearing it directly from the source is always the best.

The result of this quest is the oral history website, *VoicesofOklahoma.com*, and the book you are holding.

Since starting in 2009, I have interviewed hundreds of Oklahomans—from the famous to those who may not be as well known. All have had stories to tell—all have contributed to Oklahoma's oral history, which is the purpose of *VoicesofOklahoma.com*. In honor of our tenth anniversary, this book has been written to introduce *VoicesofOklahoma.com* to a new audience, and to provide dedicated visitors with some of their favorite stories between the covers of a book.

What you hold represents but a small portion of the informative, entertaining, and often thought-provoking interviews that fulfill the purpose of our Oklahoma oral history project. It is the first of what we hope to be several volumes of stories from *VoicesofOklahoma.com*. And while it stands on its own as a snapshot of the people and experiences that form the fabric of our state, I hope that it is also a worthy introduction to our Oklahoma oral history website.

My sincere thanks goes to the founding sponsors of *Voices of Oklahoma*: George Kaiser Family Foundation, Grace and Franklin Bernsen Foundation, H.A. and Mary K. Chapman Charitable Trust, Helmerich Foundation, The William K. Warren Foundation, and Williams Companies Foundation. Proceeds from the sale of this book will produce more stories for the website and our podcasts.

Careful readers of this book and visitors to our website may notice small differences in some of the quotes in our stories. Any changes in direct quotes have been made only for clarification and/or providing context.

John Erling
FOUNDER, *VOICES OF OKLAHOMA*

Bob Dylan, J. Paul Getty, and Will Rogers

O klahomans have earned fame and fortune in sports, in arts, and in industry—halls of fame throughout the land laud the accomplishments of Oklahomans. In addition, many Oklahomans, famous in their own right, have had more than a passing acquaintance with the rich and the famous.

For example, a renowned musician and music producer has performed with music legends such as Bob Dylan and Leon Russell, and has dined with Beatles George Harrison and Ringo Starr.

J. Paul Getty, known at one time as the richest man in the world, used to buy his suits at a Tulsa department store. Getty also helped a thirteen-year-old fledgling entrepreneur secure a bank loan. This same youngster, who would become a prominent businessman himself, watched his father buy a house from Will Rogers for $500 and groceries.

And from our "there but for the grace of God" file is the story of how losing a coin flip kept an Oklahoma musician from boarding Buddy Holly's doomed chartered airplane.

Ringo asked me, "Do you know how to run this thing?"

—STEVE RIPLEY

Multitalented singer, guitarist, guitar-maker, and record producer Steve Ripley may have yet to "see it all," but he's seen most of it—including dinner at the home of Beatle George Harrison—well, actually, castle, as Ripley told the story to the *Voices of Oklahoma* oral history website.

"I think we'd finished with the Earls Court performance," said Ripley, who was playing in Bob Dylan's band during a tour of England. "Bob is going to spend the day at George Harrison's place at the famous castle kind of thing, Henley-on-Thames, it's called. And I get the call to go. It's a dinner party. His wife's from California, and she's made a nice semi-Mexican casserole of some kind. I mean, it's all a blur.

"Jim Keltner is this drummer from Tulsa who got me the Bob Dylan gig and got me the Ry Cooder gig, you know, world's greatest drummer, in some fashion, and he's on everybody's records. For whatever reason he's always helped me, and he was helping me then. He was probably the reason I got to go. So, I'm there and it's George, and Eric Clapton had come, and Ringo Starr. At dinner, Ringo was sitting on my left. When I say it's hazy, it really is because it's unbelievable that that happened. I talked to Ringo. I said, 'Aren't you going to eat?' 'No, I'm just going to watch you eat,' he said in his Ringo accent.

"I remember we talked about shoes. He said, 'I just got these shoes, they're wrestler's shoes. I really like them.' I don't know why that sticks in my mind, but they were some kind of no-sole kind of soft shoe. It was a whole day.

"At some point, George is making us tea. And one of my favorite stories is he says to me, 'Do you take milk with your tea?' And he sees the Okie farm boy going, 'I don't know what the answer is to that.' He says, 'Well, you'll want milk with this tea.' And he didn't mean anything funny about it other than it was strong tea. He didn't wait for the answer, you know, they made tea, they made tea in George's house and he made tea for me, just me.

"And then we had the dinner and then we went up to his studio. So we did talk music at some point. And he played his latest thing that he was working on in his studio. The whole group is in the control room there, but I'm sitting at the console. I mean, I'm a recording engineer. I'm sitting at the console with Ringo, and Ringo asked me, 'Do you know how to run this thing?' And I said, 'Well, yeah, I guess I do, you know, it's what I do.' He said, 'I just don't understand it at all. The only thing that is important is what happens when the blokes get in the room.' Meaning, they get out in the big room and they start working with each other. 'That's what's important, this knob-twisting and all that stuff, I don't know anything about it.'"

That's a great memory from the farm boy who grew up near Pawnee, OK.

For more of Steve Ripley's oral history—
more great memories of dinner at George Harrison's,
touring with Bob Dylan, and other adventures in music—
go to www.VoicesofOklahoma.com.

J. Paul Getty wouldn't pay
over seventy-five dollars for a suit.
—BILL VANDEVER

I n the 1950s, Vandever's was the downtown department store to go to for everything from Paris fashion knockoffs to Levi's jeans, from a full-length mink coat to a youngster's Hopalong Cassidy outfit, and from expensive imported jewelry to Mickey Mouse watches. Five brothers owned and managed this multilevel retail space in the heart of downtown Tulsa, which was started as a dry goods store in 1905 by their uncle.

As a result, the store benefited from Tulsa's booming oil years, as well as the economic activity associated with the World War II effort. Along with that came famous customers, including one J. Paul Getty, recognized for decades as the world's richest man.

Bill Vandever managed the family business for many years, and in March 2009, he recalled one of the store's most prominent customers for the *Voices of Oklahoma* oral history website.

"Paul Getty lived in Tulsa during those years, J. Paul Getty. He owned Spartan Aircraft. In World War II he got frightened and he built a bomb shelter out where Spartan is, out next to the airport. A beautiful house he built underground. He felt that the Germans were going to bomb Tulsa."

Despite the Getty's wealth, Vandever noted, "Paul wouldn't pay over seventy-five dollars for a suit. Now, Paul was one of the richest men in America, and so when Paul came in, it was my job to go over and pull the tags off the suits that he was looking at. And then, no matter what the price was, we would charge him seventy-five dollars. And he would buy five suits at a time. Not one, not three, five. I recall he would come in like about once every year and a half or so."

Getty was not the only famous Vandever's customer, but he was unique. Sinclair of Sinclair Oil, Warren of Warren Petroleum—all shopped at Vandever's, but "they paid full price, they did. We only had to discount for one of them. And that was J. Paul."

J. Paul Getty was sitting next to him, and he heard me talking.

—HENRY ZARROW

Henry Zarrow made his entrepreneurial mark in Tulsa with Sooner Pipe & Supply—a major factor in keeping oil field operations up and humming. His success led to establishing The Anne & Henry Zarrow Foundation, which has helped thousands of Tulsans with grants to education, to make an impact on children's issues, and to assist the homeless and poor. His concern was such that when Tulsa Public Schools (TPS) were faced with a state government-induced financial crisis in the early 2000s, Henry Zarrow offered a $1 million challenge, if the public would contribute a like amount within six months. Pennies, dimes, and dollars rolled in, and the challenge was met in some three months—a tribute to Zarrow and TPS.

At the very beginning of his path to success, Zarrow encountered a man who played a pivotal role when he was just thirteen years old, but the owner of a small grocery store.

"I had the store and I dealt with the First National Bank and I've dealt with them since I started when I was only about thirteen. My loan officer was a fellow named Roscoe Adams. He was a bachelor, and he lived at the Tulsa Hotel. So I went up there at nighttime and I asked him. I said, 'I'd like to borrow $300.' He said, 'Well, you're too young, son.' I said, 'Well, yes, I know it, but I'll sure try and I hope that I can pay you. I owe some bills for groceries for my store.' He said, 'I think you are just too young.'

"J. Paul Getty was sitting next to him, and he heard me talking. He said, 'Why don't you loan the boy some money and help him get started.' So Roscoe Adams went ahead and wrote me the check."

Another brush with fame at that time was with Will Rogers.

"Will Rogers and his nephew and niece had a place at 124 East Independence. He didn't like it, but his niece and nephew did. He wanted to buy them a better place. Well, my dad was trying to buy a house, and we visited there and of course I was with my dad. The house was $2,500. Will Rogers asked my dad, 'Do you have the money to buy it?' And my dad said, 'No.' So my dad hung around another day or two, and Will Rogers used to lie out on the lawn. Everybody in the neighborhood used to be around there, and you couldn't talk business to him because he was busy talking to all of these people.

"Well, one day he asked my dad, 'Can you raise $500?' My dad said, 'Well, I think I can.' He said, 'Well, if you raise $500 and can give my nephew and niece $5,000 for a year in groceries from your grocery store, then we'll have a deal for this house.' So my dad said, 'It's a deal.' My dad raised $500, and we moved in there and we lived there at 124 East Independence for I don't know how long.

"Will Rogers was so kind and thoughtful. And I can see him now, lying out on the grass chewing on a toothpick or something with all of those people around him. It was a poor neighborhood, you know. He didn't even make my dad sign a contract or anything."

I flipped a half dollar. I said, "Call it, Ritchie."
—TOMMY ALLSUP

Tommy Allsup has a number of claims to fame—Western-swing guitarist with Johnnie Lee Wills and All His Boys, a successful career as a music producer, including Bob Wills's *For the Last Time* album—but his most lasting fame with rock 'n' roll fans and historians was due to a coin flip.

It was the winter of 1959, and Allsup was leading Buddy Holly's band, the Crickets. (The original members of the Crickets were setting out on this tour.) Holly was riding high with three recordings on the national Top 10 chart, and this tour of the Upper Midwest was planned to further his career—plus his tour mates included such stars as Ritchie Valens, who hit it big with "Donna" and "La Bamba," and the Big Bopper, who hit the charts big with "Chantilly Lace."

Allsup told the story about Buddy Holly's decision to charter a plane for three passengers—Holly, Allsup, and Waylon Jennings (who was a Cricket at the time) to the *Voices of Oklahoma* oral history website in 2011.

"The Big Bopper had the flu. He told Waylon, 'If there's any extra seats on that plane, I'd like to go with you guys.' Waylon said, 'It's just me and Buddy and Tommy that's going, but you can go in my place because I don't care about flying anyhow.' That's how come he was on it.

"Ritchie Valens had never been in a small plane before, and he asked me two or three times if he could go in my place.

"After the concert in Clear Lake, Iowa, Buddy had gone out and gotten in the station wagon and pulled it from the front of the building around to the back to the dressing room door. Buddy asked me to go in and check the dressing room to make sure nothing was left behind. That's when I saw Ritchie and we flipped the coin.

"I flipped a half dollar. I said, 'Call it, Ritchie.' He said, 'Heads.' It was heads, so I said, 'You're going.' So I went back out and told Buddy."

As a result, Allsup and Jennings got on the tour bus that night and the next morning arrived at the next stop: Fargo, North Dakota.

"We went into the hotel at about 11 o'clock in the morning. The Comstock hotel was actually right at the edge of Fargo and Moorhead. We walked in there and they were showing pictures on the TV. The road manager said, 'I'm going to check in the Winter Dance Party.' I told the guy, 'Put me in a room next to Buddy Holly.'

"The guy at the front desk said, 'Haven't you heard? Those guys got killed in a plane crash last night.'"

For more of Tommy Allsup's oral history—why it was initially reported that he had died in the crash of the plane, and how the tour went on—go to www.VoicesofOklahoma.com.

Behind Every Child

While some say it takes a village, there are successful Oklahomans who have, by circumstance and parental dedication, relied mostly upon family. Take a military family with its frequent and many moves—sometimes leaving a child feeling rootless. But a steadfast father with a love for discipline and learning can be the rock that a future success in business and life needs as his foundation. And today, every day he goes to work, a university president honors his father in a unique manner.

There is the future federal judge whose father was a horse trader and a bootlegger—but whose mother was this public servant's moral beacon. And a future governor of the Chickasaw Nation was one of six children whose father died young, yet the example set by his mother inspired him through tough times.

In Oklahoma, both father *and* mother know best.

I always wear wing tip shoes.

—JIM GALLOGLY

Throughout the years, the University of Oklahoma (OU) has demonstrated a decidedly open mind about who leads the state's flagship university. Rather than the traditional academic with numerous initials behind his or her name, OU selected US Senator David L. Boren, as its thirteenth president.

Following that precedent for president, OU's leaders turned to the world of big business and named the first chief executive officer from a Fortune 500 company as its fourteenth leader: Jim Gallogly.

A 1977 graduate from the OU College of Law, Gallogly had been in private practice in Denver prior to entering the energy business with Phillips Petroleum Company in 1980—a career path that his father had pointed him to from childhood.

As a matter of fact, Tom Gallogly, a military man who retired from the United States Air Force as a senior master sergeant, had the greatest influence on the man who would one day find success as an executive with ConocoPhillips and Chevron Phillips Chemical Company, and who would guide LyondellBasell out of bankruptcy.

His father's influence on the family of eight boys and two girls (and his mother, Margery) was evident when Jim Gallogly contributed his oral history to the *Voices of Oklahoma* website in 2018 from Evans Hall on the OU Campus.

"He was a great disciplinarian—everything had a place, everything had a rule, and he always was very, very disciplined. We had to be there at breakfast by a certain time. And when it was time to eat, you know, we had kind of an order in which people were served. We had lists for when it was our time to do the dishes and our time to mow the yard and our time to sweep the floors. There was a rule for everything. And the beds, by the way, had to bounce a quarter, or otherwise it had to be redone.

"I never saw it as irritating because it was always that way. And when you grow up in a disciplined family and you see how others may be living in a less organized way, it always seemed to me like he had a pretty good way of getting things done.

"There's a saying that sometimes necessity is the mother of invention. You can imagine what twelve people in a household with just a couple of bathrooms—we lived in a very, very modest home, sometimes on military bases and base housing wasn't very spectacular—we had to have discipline simply to get by."

But don't get the idea that the Gallogly household was run like a twenty-four-hour boot camp. As with most military families, the Galloglys were often on the move, but Jim Gallogly remembers one constant.

"No matter where we lived, he'd build a library. Just get plywood and a saw and he'd build a library. When you move a lot, you don't want to carry a lot of things, but he always had books. And he would not just have any books, he would have classic books, great books, philosophers and Shakespeare and a variety of, you can imagine, the best books. He'd always have a collection of a hundred-plus books that he would carry everywhere. And all of his children were given reading lists.

"'This year, Jim, during the summer, I want you to read these five books.' And it wasn't that we had to prepare book reports or something to prove we did it. If he said you're supposed to do something, we did it. So we'd read these books. We were never tested, never questioned—we were just expected to do it.

And it turned out that great books are a joy to read and I actually looked forward to it. Very few people could say that when they're in grade school they could write a book report about a fourteenth-century English philosopher and the book is a thousand pages long. I did that kind of thing because my father made that kind of book available.

"The other thing that was so unusual was not just the library, but it was the way he trained. My father wanted me to be a businessperson someday. I don't know why, I don't know what he saw in me, but he said, 'Jim, not only do I want you to read these books,' and he bought it, a subscription to something like *Forbes* magazine.

"And in the newspaper, he'd always save the stock market section, every day of the week. And on weekends we would chart stocks. He would have other investment books available that I was supposed to read. And we would talk about his portfolio of stocks that he owned.

"Now, it took me a long time to figure out that my father had no money and he had no portfolio, but that didn't mean we couldn't pretend. So, we had this, what I thought was a real portfolio of stocks that were in fact pretend, but if real, as poor as we were, if we didn't invest right it could make us poorer. I was very focused as a young man on picking the right stocks and understanding why, what industries, what stocks, all of that. First in grade school and middle school. By the time I got into high school I figured out he didn't own any stock and so we didn't play the game anymore. But I was learning those kinds of things."

That upbringing led Jim Gallogly to the conclusion that he lived a "privileged childhood."

"I was privileged to have a father who cared, who had great faith, who took a great deal of time and interest in each of us. He had great books for us to read, taught us discipline, showed us great examples. I mean, what a privileged environment that is. That you can't buy."

And each day Gallogly honors his father in an unusual but meaningful way.

"I always wear wing tip shoes. My father, being in the military, always had to have a shined pair of shoes. And military issue never had any decoration at all, they were just shiny black. When my father didn't have to wear those, he had on a pair of tennis shoes. But any other time, for instance going to church, he always wore wing tips.

"It's one of the things I always remember about my father was the wing tips. The reason I still wear them today—we had a trunk out in the garage. And when most people are thinking about going to school and getting new clothes for the school year, we had a different routine. We'd go out to this giant trunk in the garage, and we'd go through everything in the trunk to see what fit whom.

"In that trunk one day there was a pair of wing tips that my father had worn. They were kind of worn out but they were still very special to me, and when they would fit I wore them with great pride. And to this day, it's a great reminder of my father when I wear my wing tips."

For more of Jim Gallogly's oral history—his business career, his affection for the University of Oklahoma, and his decision to accept its presidency, go to www.VoicesofOklahoma.com.

Every day of my life I grow just a little more respectful and fond of my mother.

—JUDGE LEE ROY WEST

If you look at the paternal influence in Lee Roy West's life, there is little evidence that this man from Clayton, Oklahoma, would turn out to have such a stellar career.

(Actually, West points out that he was born in "Bobtown in Pushmataha County, but it was really just a small part of Clayton, which is pretty small itself.")

When *Voices of Oklahoma* visited with him in his chambers in the federal courthouse in Oklahoma City, Judge West looked back on more than forty years of public service that included serving as a state court judge, a member of the Civil Aeronautics Board, and a federal judge. All of this after achieving an undergraduate and law degree from the University of Oklahoma, a Master of Law degree from Harvard, and reaching the rank of lieutenant in the Marine Corps. Quite an accomplished life for a man who'd hunted "Hoover hogs" and who'd seen the sheriff haul his father off to jail.

He was fortunate that a woman from Arkansas filled the role of "moral beacon" in his life.

"Her name was Nicey Hill, and then when she married my father it became West. She was born in Arkansas near a small town called Blue Ball, Arkansas, which I have been to, but it barely exists at this time. My father was born in 1890. I guess they were married around 1910 or something like that. He had been married and been divorced," said West.

"You know, everybody thinks their mother was a great person, but my mother was truly a wonderful person. She could barely read or write. She went all the way to the third grade, but I don't think she completed that. But she was the most protective and loving parent that anyone could have, certainly that I have ever been around. She was sort of the sole moral beacon that we had in our group. My father was a bit of a philanderer and all that sort of thing. He was a horse trader and a bootlegger, but she was solid. Every day of my life, I grow just a little more respectful and fond of my mother."

Her life wasn't easy.

"She coped with the most rigorous conditions. We were very poor. They had a saying. We were too poor to paint and too proud to whitewash. I didn't even live in a home that had indoor plumbing until I went to the University of Oklahoma in 1948. We never had very much, but she coped very well to provide. I don't feel deprived at all by coming from a very poor background. My father could neither read nor write, so there was never anything in excess, but we survived amazingly well."

Among the most "rigorous conditions" was the day West's father was arrested.

The family moved all around Oklahoma during the Depression, but eventually his father sold property he had mortgaged (and failed to pay off the mortgage) and "the sheriff's office arrested my father and left my mother with four kids beside the creek out there with two horses and a top wagon and absolutely no income whatsoever.

"She was absolutely magnificent, of course. She moved us into a little cabin on an adjoining piece of land there with permission from the landowners, who furnished us the opportunity to get into the garden, and he put us to work in a sorghum mill in exchange for food and stuff like that. She hitchhiked all over southeastern Oklahoma to raise enough money to make bail for my father, and this was among friends who didn't have anything either, you know. She finally bailed him out."

Fortunately, young West had a .22 and was in a rural area so there was food on the table. He also had a good cook in his mother!

"When we were in Blanchard primarily, there was just an abundance of jackrabbits there. They had just invaded the countryside. At night, before we lost the truck, they would drive out on the prairies and just shoot washtubs full of jackrabbits. We would bring them home, and she would cook them and can them. She referred to them as Hoover hogs because they were pretty critical of President Hoover along about that time, as you might imagine. It was a pretty tough time.

"My mother was a wonderful cook, of course, and she could fix squirrel and dumplings that was as good as any chicken and dumplings that I've ever eaten. As a matter of fact, most people usually haven't eaten possum and sweet potatoes [West paused to chuckle], but we regularly ate that."

Although his father ran afoul of the law and his mother was a moral beacon, the two parents agreed on one thing and impressed that upon the young West, albeit from different perspectives. "Even though my father could neither read nor write, both he and my mother were very encouraging about me attempting to improve myself through education. My dad used to say, 'If you don't get an education, you'll wind up just like I am.' She, on the other hand, had no doubt. I had doubt, but she didn't. She said, 'You are as bright and as smart or brighter and smarter than anyone else. You can do exactly what you want to as far as getting an education.' That was very encouraging."

Encouraging, indeed. From Bobtown through Hoover hogs to a respected judicial career—all following the moral beacon from his mother.

*For more of Judge Lee Roy West's oral history—
his time spent teaching law, his courtroom experiences,
his service on the Civil Aeronautics Board, and his belief
that life should be fun—go to www.VoicesofOklahoma.com.*

You learn by example. And she did a wonderful job of providing an example.
—BILL ANOATUBBY

After his father was killed in an industrial accident before Bill had even reached the age of three years old, Bill Anoatubby's mother made sure he never forgot the father he couldn't remember.

The man who would become governor of the Chickasaw Nation in 1987 remembers how she accomplished that, along with her strength, which kept the family together and shaped his destiny. He shared these memories with *Voices of Oklahoma* in 2010 in the main conference room of the Chickasaw Nation Headquarters, located at the corner of Arlington and Mississippi in Ada, Oklahoma. His family heritage was kept alive to him by his mother, and it impacted the course of his life.

"I have no recollection at all of my father," recalled Anoatubby. "All I know is what my brothers and sisters and

Mom and other people would tell me about him. My mother would sometimes say, 'Your dad wouldn't want you to do that.' It meant a lot to me whenever she would say that."

Anoatubby was one of Opal Mitchell Anoatubby's six children—two girls and four boys—of which Bill Anoatubby was the youngest. His mother was in her midthirties when she became a widow. "She never remarried, and she raised all the kids. She worked very hard to do that. Of course, family is quite important. We all pulled together. She was not highly educated—I believe eighth grade was her highest grade that she achieved—but she had a lot of common sense and did, I think, a very good job of raising the family."

The family was helped by "insurance from my dad's passing. And I have to say a lot of good things about Social Security because there was Survivor's Insurance. It was available through Social Security. Mother also worked. I remember as a young boy she would take ironing in and did ironing so she could still be close to home. And she did various jobs. She was a cook, a very good cook, by the way, so she worked in restaurants and she did take care of some folks, caretaking, during that time. She did whatever job that she could find. She worked in a factory, something that would pay the bills."

But Opal Mitchell Anoatubby provided more than money to feed and clothe her children. She gave them a remarkable example to follow throughout their lives.

"It's amazing when I was young what they teach you, not necessarily about sitting you down and saying, 'Okay, you need to do things this way.' You learn by example. And she did a wonderful job of providing an example. She may be at the kitchen table working with her finances and I would be just a young child coming up and seeing what she was doing. She taught me, basically, through example.

"And we all learned how to work. We began working at a very early age. Either at home or outside the home, to help bring in some badly needed resources."

As he grew, education became a focus. And his mother's influence hardly waned.

"Tishomingo didn't have pre-K and kindergarten and pre-school and all the things we have today, so first grade was my first experience. I learned to read, I learned to count and all those things in the first grade. I was a good student, I enjoyed school. When the teacher said, 'Take this homework with you and do it and bring it back,' I did it. Of course, my mom had influence on that. If I had homework she made sure that I did it."

First grade and homework under his mother's supervision were only the beginning.

"When I was a senior in high school in Tishomingo, a fellow from the Bureau of Indian Affairs gathered several of the Indian students together in the principal's office and let us know about a program that the Bureau of Indian Affairs had for education: BIA education scholarship program. It actually gave me some hope. I thought, *Maybe I can do this.* So, I applied for it before I went to my active duty training in the National Guard.

"But while I was gone a letter was received from the BIA that indicated, 'Sorry, we would approve you, but we don't have any funding left.' I was pretty disappointed by that, but at the same time, I had been motivated to go. And so, I thought, *I'm going to figure out a way to do this.* I was going to attend East Central State College and then expenses were more than they were at Murray State College in Tishomingo. So, during the time I was in my six months active duty I sent money home out of my paycheck as a savings so that I could pay the tuition and buy the books when I got back.

"I was determined I was going to go, at that point. When I got back I'd saved enough for books and tuition. When I arrived to enroll at the business office and when I went to pay for the schooling, I had a scholarship and didn't realize it. It wasn't a large one, but it would have paid for the tuition. I had a little bit of extra then, and I started the college experience."

That "experience" included marriage, a renewed focus on college after an "off" year, and working at Safeway. Eventually it included a degree in accounting that led to his becoming the director of Chickasaw tribal health services and eventually the governor of the Chickasaw Nation.

For more of Bill Anoatubby's oral history—his work with the Chickasaw Nation, including the development of numerous businesses owned and operated by the Chickasaw Nation, go to www.VoicesofOklahoma.com.

An Early Propensity for Performing

There was a time when people had to pretty much entertain themselves, or find friends and neighbors who could provide entertainment. This was, of course, before radio and 600 zillion channels on television. As a result, most families had a piano or a guitar and someone who could play one or the other or both. Or without an episode of *Sesame Street* on hand to watch, a youngster might look for someplace (such as the underside of a table) to draw pictures.

Now, having a musical instrument around and a desire to play it does not necessarily make you a star. But having access to music and *talent* at a young age just might—as it did for three Oklahoma musicians. And it also turned a lad, who began drawing like a Michelangelo under his mother's table, on the road to becoming a renowned painter in his own right. Fact is, some Oklahoma artists start early.

Mother said, "You never had to ask Wanda twice to sing." —Wanda Jackson

Elvis Presley...Hank Thompson and his Brazos Valley Boys...Roy Clark...Buck Owens..."Let's Have a Party"...the Rock and Roll Hall of Fame.

Now, there is no guarantee that you'll meet, tour with, and date the biggest name in rock 'n' roll to ever come out of Tupelo, Mississippi, and be discovered by a legend in country music, and have two future stars play behind you...have a huge Top 40 hit song...and be recognized as a living legend...just because your dad bought you a guitar at an early age.

But if your dad was a self-taught musician, and if you had the looks, the voice, and the personality of a star, the rest, as they say, is history.

That's rockabilly, country-and-western, and gospel legend Wanda Jackson's story.

Born in Maud, Oklahoma, her musical adventure began in California in the early 1940s, when her family moved, seeking a better life. Her father, Bob Jackson, wanted to learn a trade, and he went to barbering school while her mother supported the family. It proved to be an unwise career choice for a man with "bad feet." But he loved music, and he shared that love with little Wanda, buying her a guitar when she was around the age of six.

She recalls that first guitar in an interview with *Voices of Oklahoma* from her home in south Oklahoma City in 2011: "It was a little child's guitar. This was the days of the war. My guitar had an Uncle Sam's hat on it and stars. We have a picture of me with that guitar."

But a guitar alone does not make an entertainer. Being surrounded by music helps. "You know, he had records, and I guess he made sure we always had a record player. So, in the evenings when he'd come in after dinner, a lot of nights we just made music and listened to music and that's why he wanted me to be able to play guitar so that he could play fiddle and I could accompany him. It didn't take me long because I loved playing, and then I began to learn some songs."

First, however, came chords, taught by her father. "I don't know how he learned, but he played all the chords right, the way they are supposed to be fingered and everything. That's all I know is that he taught me—and to sing. But my real love of music and wanting to become a singer and a performer came from the fact that they took me to dances with them. They loved to dance. On Saturday nights, we would go to the various places around L.A. I'd hear big bands like Bob Wills, Spade Cooley, Tex Williams, and the Maddox Brothers and Rose.

"The girls in those bands—after seeing them and hearing them yodel, and they were dressed in pretty sparkly dresses— I said, 'I'm gonna be a girl singer like them.' So, in my mind, the first thing I had to learn was to yodel, because all the girls in those big bands yodeled. I did that. The first thing I remember is Daddy had a big stack of Jimmie Rodgers, "the Blue Yodeler," records. Hearing those all my life, I learned the "Blue Yodel No. 6." That's as far as I know, the first song I could play the guitar and sing at the same time and yodel. So, then I was set."

Set, indeed.

When Bob Jackson's foot pain eliminated barbering as a profession, the family moved back to Oklahoma in 1953.

"Well, the first places that I sang was at church—not in the big service, you know, but for the ladies' luncheon or something

I'd sing. After church on Sunday night, the young people would go to somebody's house and have something to eat and they always wanted me to bring my guitar and sing for them, so that's how I learned to sing in front of people, plus my family—Mother said, 'You never had to ask Wanda twice to sing.' If somebody just mentioned it, I'd run and get my guitar because I liked to perform in front of people."

Her love of performing soon outgrew church services.

"There was a radio program that played a very pivotal role in my life, on KLPR. So, this disc jockey, Jay Davis, had a one-hour show and the last fifteen minutes of his show, he allowed local talent to come in and sing, so it was a wonderful showcase for all the young singers. My friends at church dared me to go up and try out. I said, you know, he wouldn't ever let me on that show. 'Yeah, I think you ought to.' After they double-dog-dared me, you know, then I had to go up. And so, Jay let me be on the show a few times and then I entered a contest on the station. Whoever won got their own radio program for, I don't know, a month, six weeks, something. I won that contest and I got a show every day after school, 5:15 to 5:30, after the news. I guess they had a way of knowing that it was pretty popular. People were listening to it a lot. We had sponsors, so when my time was up for the contest prize, they told me my show was doing good and that if I could find and keep sponsors, they would allow me to keep that fifteen minutes. That was a new phase for me, but, yeah, I got out and talked to a lumber company and a furniture company and I kept that little show sponsored for a few years."

The next big break for the teenager Wanda came when popular country artist Hank Thompson was urged to listen to her perform on the radio.

"Hank tells the story that some people had been asking him, 'Have you heard this girl on KLPR sing? We think she's really good,' and so forth, so he tuned in one day. He was in his car and he said he stopped the car when my show was over—pulled over, found a pay phone, and took the time and trouble to call me. I nearly fainted, because he was my very favorite. I did all of the Hank Thompson songs. He's still my favorite. He invited me to come sing with him at the Trianon Ballroom that Saturday night, and Hank got a kick out of the fact that I said, 'Well, Hank, I'd love to, but I'll have to ask my mother.'

"He said, 'Well, how old are you, girl?' I was either fourteen or fifteen. And he went on to be my mentor. He got me my recording contracts when I was sixteen—I signed with Decca Records, thanks to Hank. I made a demonstration record out at his home. He brought his band out and, you know, went to a lot of time and trouble for me."

*For more of Wanda Jackson's oral history—
her touring with and dating Elvis Presley, her switch
from country to rockabilly, and her career as a
gospel artist, go to www.VoicesofOklahoma.com.*

One day Dad was out doing our morning milking and I picked up the fiddle.
—CURLY LEWIS

What's in a name? According to a book on baseball cards, a name meant everything.

The point in the book was the difficulty in visualizing a man named Leonard Bernstein playing centerfield for the New York Yankees and, by the same reasoning, a fellow by the name of Mickey Mantle conducting the New York Philharmonic.

What, then, would have been the prospects for a fiddle and guitar player by the name of Julian Franklin Lewis to make it big in the music business—particularly Western-swing music? Can you hear Bob Wills leading the Texas Playboys and hollering, "Take it away, Julian"?

Fortunately, Julian Franklin Lewis not only had a "name change," but he was also loaded with talent.

He told *Voices of Oklahoma* of his name change at the legendary Cain's Ballroom in Tulsa in 2011: "Well, I had curly hair when I was a boy, and they didn't call me Curly so much until I started in the music business. After I got out and got around, I realized that Julian is kind of a bad name for an entertainer, so a lady I used to work with named Billie Walker actually said, 'Why don't you let me call you Curly?' So it stuck, and that's what I've been known as ever since."

And well known he became. As author and Western-swing historian John Wooley puts it, "There may have been one or two others, but Curly is the only musician I know who worked with four of the greatest Western-swing bands ever," the bands of Bob Wills, Johnnie Lee Wills, Leon McAuliffe, and Hank Thompson. Wooley adds that Lewis was "a giant in the field of Western swing…one of the very last of the great fiddlers who worked in the golden era; Curly was a great musician and a great man."

This great man got his start on his journey to the top when he was nine years old—and without the benefit of lessons.

"The first fiddle I ever got ahold of, my dad bought it out in Stigler for five dollars one day when he went to town. He knew an old fiddle player down home there; his name was Ed Patterson. Him and Dad had been friends for a long time, and he was an old-time fiddler player. Dad got him to come home and stay all night.

"Patterson got that fiddle out and started playing it. Now, back in those days you only went to town once a week on Saturdays. And every two or three Saturdays, why, Dad would bring him home and he'd sit there and play until midnight a lot of times. Shoot, I'd be asleep. But, nevertheless, that was how we first got our instruments."

As far as lessons, well, Curly didn't need them.

"One day Dad was out doing our morning milking and I picked up the fiddle. I hadn't even tried it before. I got to messin' with it a little bit, and shoot, I could kind of tell how it was working, you know? And I learned how to play 'Sweet Abeliena' while he was milking out there. He was out there probably forty-five minutes or an hour. He came in from milking and he asked my mother if Ed Patterson had come by. He'd heard the fiddle out there. And she said, 'No, go take a look.' He looked in there and I was sitting in there on the bed playing it. And so that's how it first came about. But it wasn't anything special to me really, it never was a very hard job to learn how to play tunes."

Within a year "my little sister started playing the mandolin and then she learned to play fiddle. She and I switched back and forth on the mandolin and fiddle. I'd play breakdowns and she'd play the songs and melodies and, I mean, singing songs and all that kind of stuff." It was a trio with his brother playing guitar.

And a year later, when Curly was eleven years old, he got his big break.

"Well, my brother, Press, was downtown fooling around, and he passed by down there where they were entering people for the fiddlin' contest that Bob Wills was putting on at the Avery Coliseum downtown. So, Press just went in there and entered me in it. I wasn't very happy about it, I didn't really want to do it. Anyway, it was a three-day contest and sixty-seven old fiddlers from seven different states and all around Oklahoma here." The third night, the sixty-seven were down to three.

"Then the three of us played off, and I was lucky enough to win it. Of course, the old saying, 'You don't perform against dogs or kids.' You know, my size had a lot to do with it, I'm sure. The grand prize was a hundred dollars. That was like, oh gosh almighty, two thousand nowadays or more, you know. I wanted my dad to take that hundred dollars and move back to Stigler because I liked that country. I was tired of town already. He wouldn't do it. Instead he bought me a blue serge suit, paid seventeen dollars for it. Boy, that was high class then."

And shortly thereafter (it was 1936), Curly made his broadcasting debut playing for the first time with Bob Wills.

"We had just come down to watch Bob Wills at Cain's, and Leon McAuliffe, Wills's renowned steel guitar player, actually was the guy that saw me up there when I came in the door, me and my brother, and he brought me down to see Bob. Bob had me get up on the bandstand and play."

John: Were you so young that this didn't bother you, or did it make you nervous?

Curly: It didn't make me nervous. I was so bashful back in those days it wasn't funny, but, in fact, I was so bashful I wouldn't even go out to the front of the stage and get my prize that night, as big as it was down there at the Coliseum. Just a scared kid, I guess.

The scared kid overcame his fear to fulfill his promise as both a master of the fiddle and guitar and as a vocalist.

By whatever name, Julian or Curly, the kid who played the fiddle at the age of ten without a lesson became a star.

For more of Curly Lewis's oral history—his experiences with four of the biggest names in Western swing, as well as what Western swing is (including breakdowns), go to www.VoicesofOklahoma.com.

I was drawing when I was tall enough to reach under the table and draw...
—CHARLES BANKS WILSON

Many great artists begin their journey to world-renowned status at a young age. Charles Banks Wilson is no exception. His "canvas" for early drawings, however, was unique by comparison.

His works have since been shown in more than two hundred exhibitions in the United States and around the world, and permanent collections of his work are found in New York's Metropolitan Museum, the Library of Congress, the National Gallery of Art, and the Smithsonian. They could also be said to be the dominant artwork at Oklahoma's State Capitol.

But to have seen his earliest works, you would have to get down on bended knee at best, and probably do a little crawling.

The Springdale, Arkansas, native, who grew up in Miami, Oklahoma, recalled his earliest artistic endeavors from his studio home in Fayetteville, Arkansas, for *Voices of Oklahoma* in 2010. He was ninety-two years old at that time:

"I was drawing when I was very, very young. I recall one time when I was drawing underneath my mother's table, which was a big area that just invited you to draw. I heard Mother driving up in the car, and I quickly erased where I had drawn and wrote instead, 'Mother, I love you' so she wouldn't get peeved at me drawing on the bottom of her table." Banks paused to laugh and added: "Any large area is always an invitation to young artists. So I was drawing when I was tall enough to reach under the table and draw, because that big area was a great invitation to draw. I was around four years old, I think."

While he showed an early interest and talent in art, his parents (his mother a schoolteacher, and his father a former big band trombone player in Chicago who settled in Miami and opened a paint and wallpaper store) did not push him in that direction. Their encouragement was more subtle than outright.

John: Would you say you maybe inherited some artistic values there?

Charles: I have no idea. You couldn't know that. My mother and father just encouraged me by giving me the tools to work with. I tell this to parents who have children that are interested in art, that my mother never did ever say, "I like this, or I don't like this." She would always say, "What do you think of it?" And for that reason, I think you have a dependence on your own attitude about your work.

John: But there must have been times when she saw a great work of yours and would say, "My, that was good."

Charles: Yes.

John: As you became an adult in the art world, she had to show you appreciation for what you had done.

Charles: Yes, yes, without saying it. She would say, "What do you think?" And I think that's good advice. But they would do such things like build me a room in their house where I could do art.

And do his art he did—and that at an early age.

"I painted Will Rogers from life when I was fourteen. I was going to draw him up on the stage in Miami. My dad made arrangements for me to go there and draw. In the meantime, instead of his being at the theater for twenty minutes, because he was getting money from the crowd, he in turn stayed almost two hours. So, in those two hours, I went back across the street and got my studio material and came over and did a painting of him. And as far as I know, that's the only painting that he ever posed for. Will Jr. and Jim Rogers said that I did the only painting as far as they know that had ever been done that way.

"He stood for me and he would do things that he was doing, and he was very nice to me. I remember I was complaining about how difficult it was doing him, and he said, 'Well, Charles, it always takes a certain amount of fleas to keep a dog from worrying about being a dog.' I loved him from that time on. I was in Florida when he died, when he was killed, and I felt like I had lost my best friend. A lot of people in America felt that way."

From drawing on the underside of his mother's table, to an early portrait of Will Rogers—Charles Banks Wilson's career path was set. Soon it was art school (paid for by his parents), a brief time in New York City, and a return to Oklahoma, where he would begin painting and meeting some of the most famous people in the world.

For more of Charles Banks Wilson's oral history—painting Will Rogers again, painting US Senator Robert S. Kerr, creating the murals in Oklahoma's State Capitol, and his encounters with Eleanor Roosevelt, Woody Guthrie, and Gene Autry (among others), go to www.VoicesofOklahoma.com.

I was around three or four years old when I first began to hear music.
—WASHINGTON RUCKER

Washington Rucker is as straightforward as the licks he plays as one of jazz's premier drummers. In his contribution to Oklahoma's oral history in *Voices of Oklahoma*, he candidly discusses issues such as shades of blackness, which kept him from a spot in a school band, to his deeply held feelings toward whites—and the evolution of those feelings over the years. He addresses his defiance of authority in high school and his ultimate "revenge," a degree from the University of Southern California (UCLA)—and the racism he and Frank Sinatra found there.

But it is doubtful that these milestones in his life, as well as working with artists ranging from Stevie Wonder and Ray Charles, to Dizzy Gillespie and gospel's Reverend James Cleveland, would have become a reality had it not been for "Crazy Red" and Mr. Dixon.

The 1998 inductee into the Oklahoma Jazz Hall of Fame shared these stories about growing up in Tulsa in the 1950s with *Voices of Oklahoma*:

John: Let's begin with talking about how you loved parades and the music of the Booker T. Washington Parade.

Washington: There was a man in the band they called Crazy Red. And he was a legendary drummer. And I think when I met him, I had to be four years old. Long before I started elementary school. The bands would come down Greenwood Avenue. They would top that hill, and the music would cascade down Greenwood and everybody would come out. So, the parades and the music itself were the two major influences that we had as a community, just the music—besides the football team and the basketball team. But it was all predicated on them marching down and playing for the football games. And I fell in love with Crazy Red. Ultimately, I got an opportunity to play in the band with him in 1952. And it was the greatest experience I ever had in my life as a musician.

John: You could say then, this interest in music started?

Washington: Right. I was around three or four years old when I first began to *hear* music. And, ultimately, when I moved on Oklahoma Street, Carver was north of me and I was right in the back of the music room of a high school and I heard music on both sides. So, I picked up my mother's black skillet, a knife, and a fork, and that was my first instrument.

John: You picked up what?

Washington: In every family on the north side of town, everybody's got a big black skillet. And I picked that up, a knife and a fork, and I began to play. I was around nine or ten when I first began to *play*.

As Rucker grew, so did his talent. Playing around with his mother's skillet quickly gave way to a maturing musical talent which was, as he explains, strongly influenced by "Crazy Red."

"Red had a cadence. I've done my own vision of what Red was all about 'cause they called him Crazy 'cause he was very inarticulate, but he played a cadence. It's a very simple cadence now that I look back on it, but then it was a thing that collected everybody. When Red played his cadence at the football games, the other team was in trouble. I always called him the twelfth man on the football team 'cause when he played it, the crowd got revved up. And when that happened, it was all over. So, he, in actuality, even as inarticulate as he was, he was able to gather people together. And you see the football players and basketball players doing this today, that's what his cadence did. They didn't have to do that; his cadence did it."

Crazy Red's influence on Rucker's playing wasn't the only area of his life in which he was deeply impacted by other men in the community. With his own father absent, he was raised by his mother with help from his aunt Margery. He looked to other men to teach him about music *and life.*

Washington: That whole thing about not having a father; I had men in my life. First was Crazy Red, and his name is James Williams, by the way. Then later it was Mr. Clarence Dixon. Mr. Dixon was a world-renowned drummer. From 1937 to 1942, he was voted the number-two drummer in the world, next to Chick Webb. Mr. Dixon basically took me in. He taught me the rudiments of how to play drums. And he was my greatest inspiration for that. He alone taught me exactly what I could do with the drums, and he said, "You know, you can take a pair of sticks and go anywhere in the world if you want to go." It has come to pass many, many times over.

Indeed, it did—to a remarkable career in a music identified with his heritage.

John: Well, why do you think it is jazz came out of the soul of blacks?
Washington: They needed an outlet. Blues is the legitimate parent of all jazz. If you hear some players play and there's a blue tonality in it, which is a note between notes, they call them "blue notes." If you don't have at least one in a forty-five-minute performance of jazz, then, in my estimation, it lacks something.

"Anybody can improvise. Bach and Beethoven improvised way back in the sixteenth century, but they weren't playing jazz. We needed an outlet. I needed an outlet, which is why I got my mother's skillet, a knife, and a fork. I got a copper drum that's worth about $3,000 to $4,000 now, only 100 were made. And when it came out, I called the company. 'Oh, Washington, yours is in the mail.' Didn't cost me a dime because of what I had done as a player. And I'm not bragging about what I've done as a player, but they respected enough about what I had done to give me that drum. I haven't bought a set of drums in probably about forty years. But the thing about it, we needed an outlet. You can only suppress a people so long."

For more of Washington Rucker's oral history—his encounters with prejudice of all kinds, his work with world-famous artists, and his movie career—go to www.VoicesofOklahoma.com.

This was about 1917 that he, William K. Warren Sr., moved to Tulsa.

—WILLIAM K. WARREN JR.

The "what ifs?" of life can make for engaging dinner or cocktail party conversation. But every now and again, there's one "what if?" that can bring all such speculation to a grinding halt. One such "what if?" is that there would be no Saint Francis Health System through the philanthropy of William K. Warren Sr. if he had not moved to Tulsa. His son, William K. Warren Jr., who carried on the family tradition of philanthropy, suggests that northeastern Oklahoma owes a tremendous debt of gratitude to a woman from Sapulpa.

"My father grew up in Nashville under very poverty–like circumstances. His father died when he was in the eighth grade, and he had to drop out of school at that time to support his mother and two sisters. And he had several jobs. He worked for the railroad there in Nashville, and he sold newspapers at the hospital there, Saint Thomas Hospital in Nashville. I'm very proud of him. He sold peanuts at the baseball game and he sold sparklers on Christmas Day. But he met a lady who was a patient who lived in Sapulpa, Oklahoma. She was in there after an operation in Nashville. And she convinced my father to move west because of the attraction of the oil and gas business that was beginning to flourish in the early 1900s. This was about 1917 that he moved to Tulsa."

Thank goodness the woman wasn't from Dallas.

Lessons in Leadership

From civic leadership, to business leadership, and even to government leadership, Oklahomans have demonstrated an ability to get things done. Often the opposition can be formidable—doubters, governmental agencies, and fellow legislators.

Five Oklahomans who have overcome the doubters, the dubious, and the naysayers share one common trait—leadership. Be it leadership exemplified by persistence, salesmanship, research, and/or strategy and tactics, five Oklahomans who have employed those qualities (some more than others, depending upon the challenge) are models of leadership with lessons for those who aspire to such a lofty role.

My drive was to put water in the river and build a canal from Bricktown to Myriad Gardens.

—RAY ACKERMAN

It is said there was a meeting of the Greater Oklahoma City Chamber of Commerce Board of Directors in 1990 that people would look back upon as a turning point in the city's history. To that statement, longtime advertising executive and Oklahoma philanthropist Ray Ackerman would emphatically respond, "That's right."

Not only was Ackerman the incoming chamber chair for 1990–1991, he was present in the meeting, which *was*, without question, a critical turning point in the city's history. Ackerman himself played a major role in pointing the city toward a brighter future.

As he recalled for *Voices of Oklahoma* in 2009 at his home in Oklahoma City, "We all went into that meeting, which was held in Seminole, with our nose a little out of joint frankly because we had lost this opportunity to have the World's Fair in 1989."

That was not the only problem the chamber was facing. For decades a mostly friendly rivalry had been ongoing with Oklahoma's second largest city: Tulsa. That former Oil Capital of the World had been on a toot since the mid-1970s, with the building of the nine-square-block Williams Center and its fifty-two-story Bank of Oklahoma Tower, as well as a new Performing Arts Center. A sparkling Main Mall had not attracted retail business back downtown, but it did bustle with downtown workers enjoying various food emporiums at noon. Plus, there were festivals galore: Mayfest, the Greenwood Jazz Festival, and the Bluegrass and Chili Festival. Why, even the PGA Golf Championship would be coming to Tulsa's Southern Hills in but four short years.

And Oklahoma City?

"We decided we were going to come up with a very ambitious plan—something that might take ten or fifteen or twenty years to execute," recalls Ackerman. "Everybody had a pet thing to talk about. Most people supported most all of the issues, but there would be somebody pushing for the new baseball park, a new sports arena, the state fairgrounds, a new civic center music hall, a new library, and a new transit system. My drive was to put water in the river and build a canal from Bricktown to Myriad Gardens. Before going to that meeting, I knew I was going to have a problem with the river because we still didn't really know if that river would really hold water."

The river in question was the North Canadian, which flows into OKC from the north, and then heads south before traversing the city from west to east.

Ackerman called on the Oklahoma City Riverfront Redevelopment Authority for the answer to his fundamental question: "We got it done, and it proved conclusively that it would hold water. So, I had that in my briefcase when I went to the meeting."

But that was just the beginning. "Anyhow, I had a little bit of a battle getting the river to be considered an issue, because people had not really thought of it that way. But the main battle also was the canal—we needed a canal."

While one particular community leader called Ackerman's proposal one of the silliest ideas he'd ever heard of (he was not alone in viewing it with less than enthusiasm), the advertising executive stuck to his plan. When the city leadership proposed a massive redevelopment package known as the Metropolitan Area Projects (MAPS), intended to rebuild the city's core with civic projects to establish more activities and life to downtown,

Ackerman's idea was a part of it. Matter of fact, Oklahoma City voters approved MAPS and added a new baseball park; central library; renovations to the civic center, convention center, and fairgrounds—*and a water canal in the Bricktown entertainment district.*

"I remember walking over to see the canal right after it opened in 1999. They put bluing in it to make it pretty. I passed this guy named Steve Collier, who was the head of the Convention and Visitors Bureau. I said, 'How does it look?' He said, 'Fantastic! I remember you bringing this idea to Seminole and I thought, *That silly SOB.*'"

Ackerman was very conscious of "branding" before anyone came up with the term, and to his mind, there was one more obstacle. He put it into specific terms: "I couldn't stand the thought of an ABC sportscaster, down the road apiece, talking about this race in Oklahoma City on the banks of the beautiful North Canadian River."

A race? Yes. On an April day in 1999, Ackerman attended the groundbreaking of the Eastern Avenue Dam of the river. He remembers, "It had rained every day of that whole week before that Friday. And on that Friday, there was not a cloud in the sky. It was a beautiful day. There was a big crowd there for the groundbreaking. There was enough water in the river that a fellow named Mike Knopp, who was an attorney and the president of the Oklahoma Rowing Association, was smart enough to have a few rowing shells in that water that rowed back and forth. I'll tell you what, the people really got excited to think that we could have rowing on the river." Today, the "canal" is an official training site for the Olympic rowing team.

But the name!

It took eleven and a half years to get the Oklahoma legislature to rename the seven miles of the North Canadian River that flowed through Oklahoma City, the "Oklahoma River."

"I kept after it all the time and the couple of bills that got introduced always got shut down, primarily because of the leadership of the rural community in Canadian County. Canadian County. They just couldn't see further than the end of their nose, you know?"

(Legend has it that when early explorers happened upon the river as it flowed from the north, well, they naturally named it after what they assumed to be its source: Canada.)

Still, Ackerman persevered.

His efforts earned him the nickname of "Old Man River." The person who coined that nickname? Following lunch on the day of the canal dedication, Ackerman passed the table of newspaper owner Edward K. Gaylord, the man who had once called Ackerman's idea the silliest he'd ever heard of. "He looked up at me and smiled and said, 'Old Man River.' That was his way of telling me he was wrong about the canal and wrong about the river."

For more of Ray Ackerman's oral history—how he eventually prevailed in getting the name of the river changed, as well as stories from his days as an advertiser and entrepreneur, go to www.VoicesofOklahoma.com.

We were able to get Bob Hope and Dionne Warwick and Kate Smith and Les Brown's band and Ed McMahon and Tennessee Ernie Ford and on and on.

—LEE ALLAN SMITH

Oklahomans enjoy a good celebration—from a backyard Fourth of July barbecue followed by fireworks, to the State's Centennial Celebration. While most citizens of the Sooner State can handle the former very well, thank you, it takes a rare flair for the spectacular and, yes, the meaningful to put on the latter.

The Oklahoma City resident who can honestly lay claim to that rare genius—the ability to plan and promote world-class special events—is Lee Allan Smith. And his behind-the-scenes magic has produced such memorable events as the Stars and Stripes Shows, Oklahoma's Jubilee, the dedication of the State Capitol dome, as well as the celebration of the Oklahoma Centennial. And Smith leaves not only a legacy, but in at least one important instance, a lasting impact.

He shared his remarkable career with the *Voices of Oklahoma* oral history website in 2009 from the Oklahoma City offices of Ackerman McQueen and Oklahoma Events. Turns out his fraternity days and air force experience served as a solid background for his life's work.

Smith's fraternity at the University of Oklahoma was Phi Gamma Delta. "I wasn't the president. I was rush chairman, I was social chairman, and I was intramural chairman. Each one of those gave me experiences that have led me to do the things that I have done. The second part of doing those things was in the air force. I have kind of created in myself the ability to try and have ideas and have vision and to frankly be a salesman of sorts.

I can't do anything well, if I have done it well, without money. And so, I have been a fund-raiser and it has turned out to be enjoyable because people still accept my calls because they were happy with the previous event and that's what we try to do."

Early on, he helped celebrate the election of a fraternity brother.

"J. Howard Edmondson was a fraternity brother, and when I got out of college I ran with him, helping as much as I could. We had a great victory party at the state fairgrounds in Oklahoma City. We had a lot of visitors coming in and a lot of movie actors and actresses from California that came in and helped.

"Later I called him. It seemed like there wasn't much patriotism, not that you have to sell patriotism. But we discussed it and he agreed to call and have May 1 through May 7 be 'Fly the Flag Week.' We bought fifty thousand little antenna flags and we did quite a promotion. We did a halftime show at the spring game in Norman. It was very, very successful. That was 1960. Later, we did a little bit bigger things for the Stars and Stripes Show that started in 1969."

Bigger? Why, of course.

"It was 1969, and you know there are people that are just as patriotic as I am and don't feel like they've got to do anything to show it, even fly the flag or wear a pin. But I was at the First Presbyterian Church one day and our minister was talking about patriotism. I just started thinking and reading a little bit. I didn't listen to the rest of the sermon very much, but I went home, and I knew the guy that had run the Myriad Convention Center and asked him to give me a call the next morning and see if it was available on June such and such date.

"That very day I even called Washington, DC, to find out about a US Army Band. It's kind of funny with the connections.

I got ahold of a guy by the name of Jimmy Rowland, who was from El Reno, Oklahoma. So for our first three shows we had the Strategic Air Command Band from Offutt Air Force Base in Nebraska. But that was just the beginning of the planning of it all. But I knew we would have to have a place to do it, and I knew we would have to have a band and I could build up from there and you had to get money to do it. But the first thing we did was to call all of the Oklahoma City broadcasters, radio and television, and formed the Oklahoma City Association of Broadcasters. So we all chipped in to do it.

"We started building that show and we syndicated it on about two hundred stations in the late 1960s and early 1970s. So, when we tried to get it on NBC, they wouldn't do it. But when they saw that most of their two hundred affiliates were NBC stations, they were getting preempted and taken off their programming. So they agreed to do it only if we sold the spots. They told me how much they would be, and we sold them all and it kind of shocked them. So, long story short, we were able to achieve network status. It was on NBC from 1969 until 1976.

"In 1976 it was a two-hour show, but we were able to get Bob Hope and Dionne Warwick and Kate Smith and Les Brown's band and Ed McMahon and Tennessee Ernie Ford and on and on. We did it on the Fourth of July the first year, and you got in free if you were wearing red, white, and blue. Later, when we were on television, we had to tape it and edit it for broadcast on July Fourth. I remember Bob Hope didn't do the show with us in 1976. He had his own show. I kidded him about this—our ratings were better than his, so that was fun."

While the show is over except for the memories, out of the Stars and Stripes Shows, Smith developed the Stars and Stripes Park.

"Well, I thought there was a lot of land space around Lake Hefner, as there is today and has been expanded by restaurants and so forth. But this particular area, I was driving down there, maybe fifty yards from the water, and my car got stuck in the mud. I didn't have a cell phone so I walked all the way home, and it was quite a little trek but that was the beginning of it, seeing this land available. So I went to the mayor, who was Jim Norick at the time. He was instrumental in getting these people at the city who had said no to change their minds. We started raising money, and we raised enough money to have fantastic equipment and picnic benches and we put a pavilion up, and we called it the Bob Hope Pavilion. There's a statue out there now and you can see the brass on it because everybody rubs his nose."

For more of Lee Allan Smith's oral history—the naming of a hippopotamus at the Oklahoma City Zoo after him, bringing the Olympic Festival to OKC, and how to fund-raise— go to www.VoicesofOklahoma.com.

For two days, all of the lawyers and the auditors and the accountants had me up and down and sideways briefing me on everything.
—JOHN H. WILLIAMS

In the mid-1960s, Tulsa's Williams Brothers Company was about as middling a company as you could find on the stock market. An international pipeline construction company that had been founded in 1908, it was well-respected, but prone to the boom-

or-bust nature of the industry, fabulously successful one year and fabulously headed straight in the other direction the next.

This was near-fatal for a publicly held company—stockholders and stock-pickers look for steady growth, predictable earnings. John H. Williams, who, along with two other family members, had bought Williams Brothers from its founding brothers, was acutely aware of this. As a result, in the mid-1960s, he began searching for an acquisition that would produce steady, even if unspectacular, earnings. Something akin to a utility company. Or a pipeline transmission company.

He found it in the Great Lakes Pipeline Company, then the largest petroleum products pipeline in America. Arranging financing for the $287 million purchase was one challenge for the small Tulsa-based company. (How small? When the transaction was completed, *Barron's* called it the case of a "minnow swallowing a whale.") But the company and its management's solid reputation lined up the needed financing. A tougher hurdle was, for lack of a better term, the deal's tax treatment. A negative decision would be a deal breaker and send the forty-seven-year-old chief executive off to find a different acquisition.

John Williams recalled that time for the *Voices of Oklahoma* oral history website in 2009 from his Tulsa home.

"We were cutting new accounting principles with the purchase of Great Lakes that were, at least from perspective of old-time accountants, considered revolutionary. We had to have one accounting for the bookkeeping that had to be agreed to by the Securities and Exchange Commission. We submitted it to the SEC staff—it had to do with depreciation. There was conflict between the SEC rules and the Interstate Commerce Commission rules, and we found a little niche we could wiggle through. It was all according to open-book standards, but it was something that the two different agencies hadn't really coordinated between themselves. We discovered that we could use it.

"The accounting staff at the SEC, when we submitted this, turned us down flat. They said, 'Absolutely, you cannot use it.' We said, 'Well, that kills the deal.' So I went to our lawyers, and I said, 'What can we do now?' They said, 'Well, there's one last thing, you can appeal to the SEC for an emergency hearing directly with the five SEC commissioners.' So we appealed and said there had to be an emergency meeting and the rules said they would answer within five days. On the third day, they told us that they would give us five minutes to present the case and that the CEO had to present the case with no accountants or lawyers, I had to do it all by myself with five SEC commissioners.

"For two days, all of the lawyers and the auditors and the accountants had me up and down and sideways briefing me on everything. I was a little scared when I went in, but I went in with the five SEC commissioners in Washington, DC, at their headquarters. What I presented was so novel and so unusual to them, that instead of five minutes they listened to me for forty-six minutes. At the end of that, they said, 'Mr. Williams, we have never heard anything like this before. It is novel, but you make a case, and if you go ahead we will not object.' That was one of the most interesting times I ever had."

The case Williams made was one that even a layman could understand, and one that swayed the SEC commissioners.

"It had to do generally with how you tax the income on the pipeline. The tax is affected by the amount of depreciation you can charge into the project, and since the pipeline that we acquired was an old pipeline that had been fully depreciated, you couldn't get much basis to depreciate it, but the ICC, the Interstate Commerce Commission, had passed a ruling that if you actually paid cash or if you actually paid for a property, you could reinstate the value up to the amount you paid for it, and that let us then develop quite a bit of annual depreciation.

"The SEC didn't realize what the ICC had done, and the SEC had never approved what the ICC had done, but they were both laws of the land that we wriggled through. Once we got that done and the Commission approved it, the next year the SEC passed a regulation that never again could this ever be done. We were the only ones that ever did it. That was the turning point, and that's what made the company."

It made the company in a big way. That was the beginning of an acquisition engineered by John Williams that grew the company from what he and his brother and cousin had purchased from its founders for $25,000, to a company with a market value of $406.5 million in 1978, the year before John Williams's retirement.

For more of John Williams's oral history—his World War II experiences as a Seabee, his early days with Williams Brothers, and the details on how he grew the company—go to www.VoicesofOklahoma.com.

During our debates on that Breast Cancer Bill, you could have heard a pin drop.

—BETTY BOYD

Betty Boyd wasn't the first woman to host a television show in Tulsa, but she clearly was the best. During her twenty-five-year career in journalism and broadcasting, her ratings and reputation were unsurpassed. She typically led the time periods of her programs first on KOTV, and later on KTUL. (She would modestly point to highly rated programs preceding and following her shows as the reason for her ratings.)

If being the ruling woman of television in Tulsa was not enough, she retired from television to write, and to take charge of public relations for Tulsa Technology Center. And then, when asked, she ran and won a seat in the state legislature.

In 2009, she paused to reflect for the *Voices of Oklahoma* oral history website on her remarkable career—beginning with the occasionally dubious joy of performing live on television.

"Lots of weird things happened in those days. I used to do the commercials for, they were called Mrs. Marshall's Pies then, it's called Bama Pies now. Paul Marshall brought the real pies down to be set up, and they had to be kind of slanted or propped up from the back or they wouldn't show because cameras were not as versatile as they are these days. He had set these pies up, and I just glanced out of the corner of my eye and the cherry pie, the filling was so good, and so full, that it broke out of the crust and it was running all over everywhere.

"And then one day on a Sears commercial, I called them Froug's (a popular Tulsa department store at the time) all through the thing. Of course, you can't take it back when you do it live.

"But the funniest one was with the little lady that I had on my show at Channel 8 who was promoting the county fair. She was from Hulbert. She looked like Mary Poppins. She was a sweet little old lady. She had a little hat on, and I am sure it must have had a little flower sticking out of the top. She was promoting the fair by telling about her craft making rugs.

"And I said to her, on live television, mind you, on camera, 'How long have you been making rugs?' And she said, 'Oh, honey, I have been a hooker all of my life.' Well, the camera started shaking. I could see on the monitor that the guys running the cameras were just having a fit. They were coming unglued, and I said, 'Oh, yes, my mother taught me to be a hooker when I was just a little girl.'"

From television, Betty Boyd moved to public relations and writing (with two books to her credit), and then...

"I was asked to run for the legislature, and I said, 'For heaven's sakes.' Just like I said about being on television. You've got to be kidding. Why would I do that? I had no political interest. I had a mixed marriage—I was in one party, and I slept with a man who was very devoted to the other party. It never occurred to me to get into politics, but I was asked to file, and I thought, 'Well, I've been here ten years at Tulsa Tech and that might be fun.' There were only seven of us in the House out of 101 when I first got elected to the House."

Her "introduction" to the State Capitol grounds was not what one would consider warm. "I was the only female House member from outside the Oklahoma City area. As such, when I tried to park when I first got down there in the House parking lot, the wonderful sergeants would come up to the window and tap on it and say, 'I'm sorry, ma'am, this is just for House members.' And I would say, 'I know.' And they would say, 'Well, are you the wife of a legislator?' And I would say, 'No, I'm a legislator.'"

One of the reasons she enjoyed serving in the legislature might have been because she was so good at it.

"I was the house author on setting up OSU-Tulsa. That pleased me very much. It originated in the Senate, and Charlie

Ford was the Senate author and I was the House author. I worked on that sucker until I thought I would go crazy. But we got it passed. It also helped all of our compass point regional universities because they all got part of the pie as well. In fact, that is how Northeastern State University is in Broken Arrow, because they all got some of the money when we started OSU-Tulsa.

"The other one, of course, that I was so pleased about was the setting up of the fund for breast cancer research and serving the uninsured or underinsured women with mammography and trying to do a lot of education about early detection. I really had to struggle with that one, but in the end, I had no struggle at all with it, because everybody but one nincompoop supported and was for that bill in the House.

"You know what the House floor looks like when we are in session? People talk to each other when somebody else is talking. They get up and go out because their constituents have called them away, or they have a telephone to answer. It's a busy, busy place. During our debates on that Breast Cancer Bill, you could have heard a pin drop. It was so gratifying. And there was only one lone hand that debated against that bill in that House, and we finally got it done.

"Don Ross and I worked really hard on a bill to help set up a fund that would assist blind people and people who had sight problems. And the other bill that I was exceptionally proud of was that I separated the Department of Rehabilitation Services out of DHS because it was a stepchild. Yes, I was pleased about that, and since I'm in a bragging mode, I never lost a bill that I got heard in committee, never."

One "secret" to Boyd's success was the goal of getting the job done with what some might consider personal affronts being ignored in favor of the larger picture. "Now, I didn't mind being called Madam Chairman, I really didn't when I was chairman of committees. That was fine. I'd rather be called chairman than chairperson, or chairwoman. I'd say, 'You can call me honey if you want to.' I don't care. That didn't matter to me."

What mattered most to Betty Boyd was getting the job done.

For more of Betty Boyd's oral history—
the World War II years, public speaking for the
March of Dimes, and her audition for her first
job in television—go to www.VoicesofOklahoma.com.

"Mr. Speaker, I move approval of House Bill 1042, to make 'Oklahoma' the state song."
—GEORGE NIGH

The legislative process can be a road filled with potholes, hairpin curves, and roadblocks. Even more so in Oklahoma. But if there ever was a bill whose sponsor assumed would pass without opposition, it was one introduced by a young member of Oklahoma's House of Representatives, George Nigh.

Nigh wanted to change the state song from a ditty called "Oklahoma, A Toast" to the title song from the fabulously successful Rodgers and Hammerstein Broadway musical *Oklahoma!* But Nigh had not figured on opposition from a fellow legislator known as "Old Man Huff."

The story, as related by Nigh—who served his state not only as a legislator, but as lieutenant governor, four different terms as governor, and as the president of Central State University—begins in 1943.

"I'm upstairs in our house in McAlester, no air-conditioning. I'm lying on my bed, windows are open, and I got the radio on. I suddenly sat up and said, 'They're singing about my state.'"

Nigh told this story to the *Voices of Oklahoma* website in a 2009 interview at the Cherokee Yacht Club on Grand Lake. He continued reminiscing about falling in love with the song as a teenager: "I can remember exactly the first time I ever heard this song, 'Oklahoma.' Back in those days, they had Lucky Strike's *Your Hit Parade* every Saturday night. They counted down the ten most popular songs in the nation. Four or five songs from a stage play about our state made number one on *Your Hit Parade*. It's the best-known state or country song around the world to this day.

"I'm just this kid in high school, and I said, 'Wow.' Little did I know then, I would go to the legislature in 1953, ten years later."

First elected as the youngest member of the state legislature in 1950, Nigh introduced his bill to make "Oklahoma" the official state song in 1953.

"So, in '53, I decided that I wanted the image of Oklahoma to be like the stage play. I introduced the bill to change it from 'Oklahoma, A Toast,' to 'Oklahoma,' from the stage play. I was teaching Oklahoma history. I thought it'd be a piece of cake."

However...

"A guy I call 'Old Man Huff,' who also taught Oklahoma history, I think over in Ada, he took the position to oppose my bill. I couldn't believe it. There was only one microphone in those days in the legislature, and he got up and he started hollering and screaming and preaching. He said, 'I can't believe you're going to change a song that was written by a pioneer, steeped in tradition and couched in history, and you want to change it to a play written…' I won't forget this phrase, 'You want to change it to a play written by two New York Jews who've never even been to Oklahoma? And they say, "taters and ter-may-ters?"

"I'm looking around, and he is making this impassioned plea and he says, 'This is our song.' He starts singing 'Oklahoma, A Toast.' He leaves the microphone and starts walking on the floor singing, 'Oklahoma, Oklahoma, fairest daughter of the West.' He gets the legislators by the arm and makes them stand. 'Oklahoma, Oklahoma, it's the land I love the best.' He just walks all over the legislature, and he's still got the floor, and so I can't interrupt him. He starts crying. Tears are coming down his cheeks.

"Anyway, I looked around and I saw that bill going down the toilet.

"I asked for unanimous consent to postpone consideration of that legislation for one legislative day. Old Man Huff didn't catch on to what I was doing. He didn't object to delay it. That meant I could bring it up the next day.

"I got on the phone, and first I got the state representative from Chickasha. The college there used to be the Oklahoma College for Women and its chorus was all girls. I said, 'Can they sing "Oklahoma"?' He said, 'Yeah, we just did that production not too long ago.' I said, 'I want your girls choir up here tomorrow. They're going to perform music from *Oklahoma!* on the floor of the legislature.' He said, 'I'll get them there.'

"Then I got on the phone and called Ridge Bond, who then lived in Tulsa. Who's Ridge Bond? Ridge Bond is the only Oklahoman ever to star as Curly on Broadway in *Oklahoma!*, but more important than that, he graduated from McAlester High

School. Ridge Bond was in high school with my brothers and I was just a little bit behind, so I knew Ridge Bond from McAlester. I called Ridge in Tulsa and I said, 'Ridge, you still got any of those *Oklahoma!* costumes?' He said, 'Oh yeah.' I said, 'I want you down here tomorrow. You're going to sing "Oklahoma" for the legislature.' He said, 'When are we going to rehearse?' I said, 'There ain't no rehearsal.'

"There was a music company called Jenkins Music Company in Oklahoma City, so I called them, and I said, 'This is State Representative George Nigh. You got any legislation you're really interested in?' They said, 'Yes, we do.' I said, 'I need a piano.' They said, 'Okay, Representative Nigh.' They sent out a piano.

"The next day, I get up on the floor of the legislature and I said, 'Mr. Speaker, I ask unanimous consent, the privileges of the floor will be given to the girls' chorus from Oklahoma College for Women and to our friend, Mr. Ridge Bond of Tulsa, Oklahoma.' No one objected. The girls' chorus came in and they sang 'Oh, What a Beautiful Morning,' and they sang 'People Will Say We're in Love.' They did sing all those things.

"Then suddenly, the piano player started that, 'Boom-boom-boom-boom, boom-boom-boom-boom,' coming up from the bottom of the piano—the lower keys. Ridge Bond, in his Curly outfit, kicked open the doors into the legislature with his cowboy boots and his thumbs in his belt and his hat on his head, and he came in and he started singing, 'Oklahoma, where the wind comes...' and the legislators stood and cheered and applauded as they sang 'Oklahoma.'

"The entire crowd in the gallery, all two hundred of them, stood. Of course, I had put them up there. I had gotten all the secretaries to come in and sit up there, and they stood and cheered.

The whole crowd sang 'Oklahoma.' Then Ridge ended the song with 'O-K-L-A-H-O-M-A, Oklahoma. O-K, yeow!'

"Then I said, 'Mr. Speaker, I move approval of House Bill 1042, to make 'Oklahoma' the state song.' And it passed."

And that's a story about the legislative process you'll never find in any book on political science.

For more of George Nigh's experiences as governor during the campaigns to legalize horse racing and liquor by the drink, as well as his efforts to boost Oklahoma tourism and his lifelong love for Oklahoma, go to www.VoicesofOklahoma.com.

The Entrepreneurs

There is the college graduate who was considering graduate school and a career in teaching, the dime store manager who had visions of owning his own store, the piemaker who sold a hamburger titan his wares, and a successful insurance business owner who thought a store concept he saw in Dallas might work in Tulsa. Four disparate individuals—each who had an idea that in some cases came through thoughtful planning, or in one case, appeared suddenly.

From a single product to a Hobby Lobby retail store, from a couch to a Sunday exploration that resulted in Eskimo Joe's, from a meeting in Chicago to selling single-serving pies across the country, and an idea that found the right man to make it happen—Oklahoma entrepreneurs have made their mark.

I thought I might enjoy teaching at the college level.

—STAN CLARK

Oklahoma State University College of Business graduate Stan Clark was having a heck of a time landing a job in 1975. That should not have been the case for a graduate with a 3.8 grade-point average. But there was one small problem. During the typical cliché-ridden job interviews he was suffering through, he kept responding honestly to the question, "What do you want to be doing in five years?"

"Well, basically, I've always wanted to work for myself," he would reply.

Which, basically, is why, two weeks after graduation, he was lying on a couch at a friend's house watching reruns of *Star Trek*.

His career plans at that time? "I thought I might enjoy teaching at the college level. Because I did enjoy the academic experience, and I very much admired the OSU professors. I actually had a graduate assistantship lined up and intended to pursue an MBA right after school because I did not get any job offers."

Clark, the cofounder of one of the country's most fabled bars and restaurants, Eskimo Joe's, also told *Voices of Oklahoma*, from his corporate office in an old Victorian home in Stillwater in 2012, why he was so up-front with job interviewers about his entrepreneurial ambitions.

"When I was in the fourth grade my dad, Emerson Herbert Clark, formed his own company and became the president of Distribution Construction Company. In the context of my life I really saw what it meant to watch my father going from being an employee to being an owner," Clark said.

"At any rate, my father instilled that in me from very early on. We talked about it often. There was no doubt when I came to Oklahoma State University years later and went into the College of Business that I was thinking of how I would apply those principles to my own business."

Applying those principles would not come until some five years after graduation, but his chance came with a swiftness and a lucky break that confounds imagination. You can't make stuff like this up.

Clark related the details to *Voices of Oklahoma*: "Two weeks after graduation on a Sunday I'm lying on the couch at my future partner Steve File's house watching reruns of *Star Trek*. File walks in and goes, 'Hey, Clark, I'm going to open a bar.' I go, 'Gee, File, it's a great idea. I know all these bars around here are doing great. I know where there's this cool little two-story building for rent. I'll go in partners with you.'

"So immediately I jump up off the couch and we got into his 1953 Chevy and drove about four or five blocks around the campus to what's now Eskimo Joe's. And I always say, 'As fate would have it, the owner of the property was there that Sunday afternoon.' He was a gentleman by the name of Dave Lambert. Dave had a construction company here in Stillwater. He had been the mayor of Stillwater, very long-standing family name here in this market, in this town. He and a marketing professor by the name of Bob Hamm had just bought this building.

"We walk in, we're looking around, we're thinking it's pretty neat. Very unusual old building, very stately kind of stone. Had a little cornerstone on it, '1938.' We just thought it was neat. We expressed our interest.

"The owner said, 'Well, fellows, if you want it just like you see it, I need $350 a month. If you want me to put air-conditioning in it for you, I'd need $400.' Steve and I look at each other and say, 'We're going to need air-conditioning. Let's go with that.' We shake hands and that's the inception of Eskimo Joe's. I mean, it literally happened in about a fifteen-minute window on a Sunday afternoon in May of '75."

And it happened because a father had passed on the virtues of entrepreneurship, because of Stan Clark's total honesty during his postgraduate job interviews, and due to whatever one wants to call the coming together of the interested parties at a place previously known as "Foos Roost"—that's "Foos," as in "foosball"—on one Sunday afternoon in Stillwater, Oklahoma.

That's hardly the end of the story, for there's the financing, the bank loans for a bar coowned by a twenty-one-year-old (and the trust of the banker who extended the loan), the remarkable Eskimo Joe's logo, and more, to be found at www.VoicesofOklahoma.com.

I was sitting at the lunch counter at Penn Square that had a TG&Y with two fellow managers, and we were just sitting there talking.
—DAVID GREEN

David Green is a business success by any standard.

From an initial bank loan from a bank that ended up failing (perhaps it should have loaned him the additional $1,000 loan he sought after paying off the $600 loan), Green built the hugely successful Hobby Lobby to more than 800 stores nationwide with the headquarters building in a 3,400,000-square-foot manufacturing, distribution, and office complex.

A remarkable accomplishment for anyone. Particularly anyone who'd picked cotton near Altus, Oklahoma, on weekends to supplement his pastor father's income, who had to take the seventh grade twice, and who was so reluctant to give an oral book report that he readily accepted an F rather than speak in front of his class.

But those were not barriers to David Green. His high school had a distributive education program, which allowed him to attend classes until 11:00 a.m. and then go to work—and this was where he received an advanced degree in retailing from a man called T-Texas Tyler.

"My junior and senior year, I was out of school by 11 o'clock and I was working about forty hours a week at the local five-and-dime store," Green told *Voices of Oklahoma* in 2009. "I wasn't that interested in school, but when I got to work at McClellan's five-and-dime store in Altus, I just really took to it. I really, really enjoyed being a stock boy and building displays.

"We called my boss T-Texas Tyler. And Mr. Tyler took special interest in me and gave me a lot of training. He would work with me and take me down and buy me a Coke at the local drugstore. There I was, I was interested in the retail business and he was interested in me, so it really worked well for me to learn from the manager of the store.

"There was just something fascinating to see the goods and I'd see the cost when I'd check merchandise in, and just seeing the economics of buying and selling products. And how you could display it and how the display made a lot of difference as to how fast or how well you sold the product. So I just found that very fascinating.

"I know that through the years—and I've been in retail now over fifty years—it's always very, very exciting to me. It started at that very young age. I don't know if I would have been as interested if someone hadn't taken personal attention to me and given me the time that Mr. Tyler did."

Green's ambition was to become a McClellan's store manager, but the slow growth of the company limited management opportunities, so Green made a change.

"TG&Y was the Walmart of their day back in the early '60s; they were adding seventy, eighty stores a year. They were growing with leaps and bounds. I knew that if I came over to TG&Y I could become a store manager a lot quicker because of their fast-paced growth, so I came over to TG&Y. My first position was in Shawnee as an assistant manager. I was about twenty, yes, because as soon as I turned twenty-one, after I had been with the company for six months, they gave me my first store to manage, which would be 1962.

In 1970, "I was sitting at the lunch counter at Penn Square that had a TG&Y with two fellow managers and we were just sitting there talking. One of them said, 'We ought to get into business and make clocks.' I said, 'Well, if I'm going to make something, I don't want to make clocks. I want to make little miniature frames, because here at TG&Y I can't find any of them. There's a fad right now with people buying these little frames that have canvas in them.' The customer would paint on the canvas and they would put four or five of them in a grouping on a wall.

"We didn't know how much money it would take. None of us had any money. It took all (the money) we had to support our families. *So, we thought, we'll just go next door to Penn Square Bank and we will borrow the money.* One of the three said he didn't want to gamble the $200, so he wouldn't go with us, so a guy named Larry Pico went with me. We went to the bank and borrowed $600 to start Greco, which was a combination of our last names, Green and Pico.

"We didn't have a hard time borrowing the money because of our jobs. We spent $450 of that for a chopper that would miter the moldings, and we spent the other $150 buying the moldings. Well, we didn't read any directions or anything. So, we put this in our garage and we came up with just about a dozen little samples of frames to give to a salesman that had a lot of lines. He not only had our line, but he had a lot of other lines. In about a month, he came back with $3,500 worth of orders. Well, we had no money left."

Fortunately, Greco found a company to fulfill the orders on credit, and the little company was off and running, so to speak. A first retail store was opened in 1972, but it was a struggle; with Green continuing to work for TG&Y, his wife, Barbara, had to keep the new business going.

"She worked for the first five years without pay. There were many, many times that we would ask what are we doing this for. You know, it's hard and we are crawling. There are a lot of very, very difficult times when you start with no money at all, or almost—$600 was not a lot to start what is now a $2 billion company.

"By that time, we had all three children. In fact, she would take our youngest daughter down in her carrier and take her down to ship frames. My daughter would be in a little rocker or something while she was shipping frames. So, she took care of the home, because I was working for TG&Y probably sixty or seventy hours a week. She is the reason why we're here today because it couldn't have happened without her free help. That was the only way we could have survived because there was no money to pay anybody to do otherwise."

Faith, hope, and $600—today a $2 billion company.

For the details on how Hobby Lobby grew, the bank that turned him down for a $1,000 loan, and his buying out of the "co" of Greco, go to www.VoicesofOklahoma.com.

He went up and met with Mr. Ray Kroc of McDonald's.
—LILAH MARSHALL

There was a time, believe it or not, when a business deal could be done without layers of lawyers and dozens of documents. One businessperson would propose a deal to another, there would be a handshake, and both would profit.

That was how a small pie-making business in Tulsa vaulted into national prominence: a handshake.

Paul Marshall and his wife, Lilah, moved to Tulsa in 1937 and began a pie-making business. She recalled, in 2009 for the *Voices of Oklahoma* oral history website, how Bama Pies (named after her mother-in-law's middle name: Alabama) grew. "We had no idea we were building a major company. We just did what we had to do."

She continued, "We made pies just for grocery stores. They were about six- or seven-inch pies, little fruit pies. They were not even fried pies, they were baked pies. Fried pies came along a little bit later and they just swept the baked pies off of the market. We didn't even make baked pies anymore."

Paul Marshall was in Chicago and saw a pie truck with "frozen pies" on it, "and he got the idea that that's the way we ought to go. He could see the future of frozen pies. And that's when we started developing frozen pies in our line."

Marshall landed the Howard Johnson's Turner Turnpike restaurant business and then went back to Chicago to meet with the head of a growing hamburger chain.

"He went up and met with Mr. Ray Kroc of McDonald's. And they just hit it off. It was something that McDonald's needed, and Paul just happened to approach them at the right time. Kroc was a very outgoing. He was really likable, and he was a good salesman and he was smart."

After first being test-marketed in Joplin and Springfield, "they did so well that they did not hesitate about putting them on the market."

But Marshall needed $250,000 for the equipment to gear up to supply McDonald's. It was 1966, and "Kroc came down and helped us get the loan. He went to the bank for us. He went there and stood for us, you know, McDonald's did.

"They never signed a contract. It was a handshake. We never had a contract. It was just on our word and their word. I mean, we either please you, or we are out."

Bama is the McDonald's pie supplier to this day.

For more of Lilah Marshall's oral history—why the company's product is called "Bama," why fried pies replaced baked pies, and how the company grew, go to www.VoicesofOklahoma.com

I was standing in front of the Philtower building in downtown Tulsa one May afternoon.

—BURT B. HOLMES

Had it not been for a chance encounter with an acquaintance from Woodrow Wilson Junior High School, Chester Cadieux would not have become a cofounder of one of the most honored and respected names in the world of convenience stores: QuikTrip.

And while chance can play a role in many lives, rare it is when it steps up to the plate and knocks a home run out of the park. Which is what happened in 1957.

The man with the idea—Burt Holmes, who ran into the man who implemented his idea, Chester Cadieux—recalls that time in 1957 for *Voices of Oklahoma*.

"I had gone to junior high school with Chester at Wilson Junior High School. Later, he went to Central High School and I went to Rogers. We didn't see each other again until after we both had graduated from college. We met at a wedding. I got to know him then. He was in the air force at the time. And he came back and he went to work. He tried to sell printing and he wasn't very good at it.

"I was standing in front of the Philtower building in downtown Tulsa one May afternoon. And I saw Chester coming down the street. Of course, he's only about five six, you know. And I looked down at him and I said, 'You look awful, Chester.' He said, 'Well, Holmes, you don't look much better yourself.' I said, 'Well, let me tell you my problem.'

"So, I took him inside. There was a place called the Tower Grill at that time. It had great malts. I bought him a malt and told him that I had this idea. I'd been down to Dallas and seen the 7-Eleven stores and I thought there needed to be something like it in Tulsa."

Holmes, a University of Tulsa graduate who had built a successful insurance company, told of trying to convince another Tulsa businessman to join him in making Holmes's idea a reality in Tulsa. But, after a year of trying, his idea was only that, an idea. Holmes was firmly committed to bringing the convenience store concept (even though at that time it did not have that name— they were call bantam stores) to Tulsa to the point he had signed a letter agreement for a lease on space.

He told Cadieux what he was up to and said, "A friend of mine at the bank across the street is going to loan me $5,000. I've got three guys who want to put up 2,000 bucks apiece. And I'm looking for someone who will put up $5,000 and I'll let him run the company."

"Chester said, 'I hate what I'm doing. I might like to do that.' I said, 'Well, look, I'm leaving town for a week. When I come back I'll check with you.' He said, 'I'll talk to my dad and see what he says.' So, he came back and his dad told him he'd loan him the $5,000, and that's how it got started.

"It was about that simple."

It was also simple from the standpoint that it fit into what Chester Cadieux, who had a degree in business administration from the University of Oklahoma, had in mind for the kind of business he wanted to be in.

Speaking to *Voices of Oklahoma* from QuikTrip's corporate offices in Tulsa in 2009, Cadieux recalls, "Well, Burt Holmes had asked two or three other people if they would like to be the president of QuikTrip and work the night shift and, you know, get started and all that sort of thing. All of them had better jobs than I did and they didn't want to do that and I just jumped on it. I mean, it was like…because I had these rules: It had to be simple, because I didn't know anything. It had to be low-cost, because I didn't have any money. And I didn't like competition, because if you're a printing salesman, everybody in the world had a printing press in their garage. I mean that's a dog-eat-dog business. And I didn't want to get into something with real tough competition because you couldn't survive.

"And here comes Burt. Duh!"

Cadieux's "duh" was one of "where has this been all my life?"

John: Did you try to maintain an investment and try to start this business while you were still working at the print shop?

Chester: No, no, they fired me because they did business with one of the companies that was doing what I was doing. So, then Burt decided that they could pay me while we were getting a store opened so we didn't starve.

Cadieux wasn't sitting idle while the store was being prepared. He went to work in grocery stores over the summer "just so I could run a cash register and know about groceries and knew how to order and how to stock and how to, you know, it was pretty simple. But I worked all summer in various and sundry grocery stores. We had figured out who our wholesaler was going to be and the wholesaler arranged it."

There was another lesson learned soon after opening the first QuikTrip in a strip center on the west side of Peoria south of 51st Street. "We didn't understand what we were getting into, absolutely. We stocked it like a grocery store. Which was not atypical then because we were filling a gap in grocery stores' hours. They were open from 8 a.m. to 8 p.m.; they weren't open early, they weren't open late, and so your fill-in business before 8 a.m. and after 8 p.m. was kind of what you lived on because we kind of really just had groceries."

A final lesson learned is how circumstance can dictate outcome. As Burt Holmes relates the story of running into Cadieux on a Tulsa street he also recalls that Chester was not on the list of people he was planning to call to implement his plan. "Would I have called him? No. It was absolutely fortuitous for him and me that we saw each other that day."

For more of the Burt B. Holmes and Chester Cadieux story (and how Quick Trip became QuikTrip, how Cadieux turned around the fledgling operation, and other adventures in the C-store business, go to www.VoicesofOklahoma.com.

He would pay for his way by stamps ... put himself on a mail plane.
—COKE MEYER
ON HER GRANDUNCLE WILL ROGERS

For a man who helped promote civil aviation and its benefits, who counted among his friends Wiley Post—the first pilot to fly solo around the world—Will Rogers was not instantly enamored with flying.

As his grandniece Coke Meyer recalled for the *Voices of Oklahoma* oral history website from the lodge house at the Will Rogers Memorial, "The first time he went up in Washington, DC, he said he could barely open his eyes and look around, he was so scared. But he overcame that pretty quickly."

Indeed, the man who said, "My ancestors didn't come over on the *Mayflower*, but they met the boat," became so dedicated to flying that he developed a unique method of getting from one place to another long before regularly scheduled commercial flying became commonplace.

As Coke Meyer tells it, "The government gave him rights to fly on mail planes. He would pay for his way by stamps and weigh himself in with his overcoat and his typewriter. He always carried that typewriter, an old beat-up Underwood in a little case. He would always pay for all of that and put himself on a mail plane."

A wholly original version of air mail—special delivery.

Law and Order
in Oklahoma

With a heritage as one of the last outposts of the wild and wooly west—six-shooters were common on the hips of citizens in the Indian Territory—Oklahoma is no stranger to crime. Names such as the Daltons and the Doolins on one side, and Heck Thomas and Bill Tilghman on the other still have a bit of mystery and intrigue about them.

Although most people would say that crime today has become much more sophisticated, fact is that a gunshot (or two) were central to three of the state's most famous crimes—and, thankfully, no shots were fired during a famous fourth. A victim, and a cross section of Oklahoma lawmen, relate their unique perspectives concerning four famous examples of law and order in Oklahoma.

When you got a murder and you just got two
people there, one of them is dead and one
of them don't talk, you got a problem.

—SHERIFF GEORGE WAYMAN

ON THE MULLENDORE MURDER CASE

It is an unsolved case that shouldn't be unsolved. After all, one of the state's most renowned investigators, Sheriff George Wayman, was on it.

But before he could begin his investigation, the crime scene was "botched." As Sheriff Wayman, now retired and ninety-one years old in 2014, put it, "Everything went wrong from the beginning."

The body had been removed and taken to the hospital. The victim "had a hole in the back of his head that was that big. Wasn't no life there, he was dead. You wouldn't have to be a medical examiner to tell it. So, there wasn't any reason to rush him to the hospital," recalled Sheriff Wayman for the *Voices of Oklahoma* website.

And then the body was moved to a funeral home. "We get to the funeral home, and I said, 'Now, don't do anything to his body. Leave it like it is, don't wash it, don't do anything.' Well, they cleaned up the body. The funeral home did."

Despite that rocky start, Sheriff Wayman's investigation did reach a conclusion—a theory about the crime known as the Mullendore Murder Case, or the Murder at the Cross Bell. A murder that has become so legendary that books were written about it.

The essential facts are that E.C. Mullendore III, thirty-two years old and deeply in debt, was murdered on September 26, 1970, at his home on the largest ranch in Osage County, Cross Bell Ranch. The murder happened on a night after deputies had been trying to serve divorce papers on Mullendore.

There was a $15 million life insurance policy on E.C. Mullendore III, which would become the largest life insurance claim in the history of American underwriting. Chub Anderson—personal assistant to E.C. Mullendore III—was in the house at the time of the murder and became the prime suspect.

Talking to *Voices of Oklahoma* from his home in Fairfax, Oklahoma, Sheriff Wayman shared his theory on what happened. "E.C.'d been drunk for months, and him and Chub was fussing. And Chub had about all of it he could take. Chub was mean.

"When they go in the house, I think E.C. got his pistol out, an old .38, army-style pistol with a ring in the butt of it that he kept in his van. And I think he shot Chub in the shoulder. E.C. shot Chub in the shoulder.

"Then I think Chub took that pistol away from him, beat him to death, and then shot him. Chub always carried a .25, a good ol' .25 pistol. And he'd made up the story where he shot through those glass doors at the getaway man."

John: Well, the story that Chub said when he was questioned about this was that he was actually upstairs.

George: That didn't pan out. I'm telling you what I think happened. Chub said he was upstairs drawing bathwater, and then he said he heard gunshots downstairs. Then Chub says that he goes downstairs, and he was looking over E.C., and that's when he says he got shot in the shoulder.

John: And you believe that shot actually came from E.C.

George: Yeah.

John: And then when he turned, he says he saw two intruders run out the glass doors and he shot at them and, of course, didn't hit anybody. I guess the question would be that if they were there to shoot E.C., why wouldn't they shoot Chub as well?

George: We dry-runned that again just like Chub said it happened. It didn't work that way. You couldn't hear that bathwater running upstairs, you couldn't hear the shot down there. We dry-runned it time and time again. That what Chub said didn't happen. It was a case, if everything would have gone right, it would have been worked before daylight.

John: You would have had it solved before daylight?

George: Yeah. If the body hadn't been moved, they hadn't cleaned up the body, it'd have been worked before daylight.

John: How would you have tied Chub to it?

George: Just like I'm saying here. When you got a murder and you just got two people there, one of them is dead and one of them don't talk, you got a problem. We had to prove what he was telling us didn't jive with what happened. I think Chub had a 50-50 shot of being found innocent because E.C. didn't have too good a record, you know. Lots of people didn't like him. He had trouble with a lot of people. He was in financial trouble, and you could line that wall three times up and down there of people who had a reason to kill him.

No one has ever been charged with the murder.

For more of Sheriff George Wayman's oral history about the Mullendore case, including E.C.'s funeral, the divorce issue, the life insurance policy, and his confrontation of Chub Anderson, go to www.VoicesofOklahoma.com.

I thought he was probably going to kill me.
—WALTER HELMERICH III

The life of Walt Helmerich III had a storybook quality to it—right up until a day in June of 1974, when the storybook tale threatened to turn into a nightmare.

He was planning on a career as a teacher until, in 1950, he met movie star Peggy Dow (who played a role in the movie *Harvey* with Jimmy Stewart, among other films and costars). Meanwhile, his father, Walter H. Helmerich II, prompted him to attend Harvard Business School, and later to join Helmerich & Payne.

With wife, Peggy, at his side, he turned the company's wildcatting business practices into a leading worldwide contract drilling firm with assets that included Tulsa's famed Utica Square Shopping Center (a onetime general-purpose shopping center that Helmerich transformed into an upscale shopping experience).

As his wealth grew, so did his philanthropy—the Universities of Tulsa, Oklahoma, and Oklahoma State were among the higher education recipients of his generosity, along with public schools, parks and playgrounds, the Gilcrease and Philbrook Museums, and other statewide interests, including the *Voices of Oklahoma* website, whose founding depended on his support.

But the story could have had an unhappy ending on a day when Walt Helmerich was taking his usual morning drive to work.

He recalled that day for the *Voices of Oklahoma* website in 2008 in the boardroom of Helmerich & Payne in Tulsa.

"I always drove to work the same way every morning, down St. Louis Avenue to the Utica Square area. Going down the street, this guy a half block ahead of me jumps out in the street with a stop sign. He had on an orange jacket and he was wearing a hard hat. He was just standing right in the middle of the street just waving this sign.

"I pulled up to him and I stopped. He comes around to my window. One of the things I'll never forget, he had a Band-Aid over his top lip and another one over his lower lip, just a Band-Aid. He said, 'There's a gas leak ahead and you've got to stop until it clears.' I said, 'Okay.' So, I leaned over to turn off the ignition and I felt this cold gun in the back of my... He said, 'Now do what I tell you or I'm going to kill you.'

"I said, 'Look, I will give you everything I have.' He said, 'No, that isn't what I want. Just get over into the passenger seat.'

"So, we go driving off. He said, 'Keep your head down between your knees. I don't want you looking up, and I don't want you looking at me.' So, we drive. I didn't know it, but we were in that underground parking that used to be on the south side of Utica Square, where the doctors parked. We must have gone way back in the corner. He said, 'Now, get out.'

"He put me in another car, but before he put me in there, he taped my hands, interestingly, in front of me. He put a blindfold on me. I couldn't tell what it was, but it turned out to be a Roy Rogers mask, but he taped the eyeholes. He put that across my face and taped it. Then he pushed me into the back seat of his car, thank goodness it wasn't the trunk, and he taped my feet together. So, I was lying on the floor. He covered me up with something. It was a huge piece of material. I always thought it might have been a parachute or something. We started driving off.

"He had told me during the drive, after I was put in his car, that he wanted $700,000 or he was going to call my dad. I said, 'Look, my dad has had a heart attack recently. If you tell him this, there is no telling what will happen.' He said, 'Well, what do you think?' I said, 'Call my banker. That's who's going to have to put the money together for you. He's across the street from my dad. He'll be able to go over and soften the blow anyway.' He said, 'Okay, I will do that.'

"So, he called Vic Thompson, who was a good friend of mine. I knew from being on the First National Bank Board that any threat to a bank, they immediately call the FBI. He calls the office after I told him to give Vic time to get over there. I told him to call the office and ask for Dad. Dad knew all about it by then. He told him what he wanted. He said, 'I'm going to give you an address. I want you to go there and use the pay phone. You go there, and I will give you further instructions.'

"There were three FBI guys involved by then. Within three hours, there were FBI officers from Kansas City, Wichita, Oklahoma City, Dallas, and Fort Worth. The guy that came up from Fort Worth was their sniper. Peggy was listening to all of this on the radio with our boys. The sniper asked what rifle he needed to bring and what scope, you know, because of what distance.

"Dad started out and got lost. The guy said to me, 'Your dad hasn't shown up. What does this mean?' I said, 'Look, he's probably scared to death. Just call back to the office.'"

Helmerich's secretary went with his father on the second attempt to make the "drop." And eventually: "At the second place they had agents all around. They spotted this car that had been in the first place drop. So, they assumed that it was the guy who had me. They started tailing him. Then he went to three more phone booths around town. They still didn't know where I was, and they wanted to try to find me. They said that almost always these guys work with an accomplice and they keep the kidnapped person where the accomplice is. If they pick up the guy in the car, he'll say, 'Look, we'll kill him.'"

Through it all, Helmerich had something that kept him calm.

John: Weren't you panicked at any time?
Walter: No, because when he put the gun to my head, I said, "Lord, I'm going to hand this over to you because I can't handle this kind of situation." So, I really never was afraid.

Anyone of lesser faith would have been afraid, particularly when the ransom money was in hand and the kidnapper "kind of dragged me out because my feet were still tied, and he just dragged me out and pulled me out on the road. That's when I knew that this was probably the end. I thought he was probably going to kill me."

For more of Walt Helmerich's oral history—more kidnapping details and how he was ultimately found, his marriage to Peggy Dow, building Helmerich & Payne, and his civic involvement, go to www.VoicesofOklahoma.com.

———

She was a bootlegger, there was no question about that.
—S.M. "BUDDY" FALLIS

It is rare that a lawbreaker's funeral is attended by a congress-man, a district court judge, a state senator, and a contingent of city and county law enforcement officials.

But such was the case in Sapulpa, Oklahoma, on February 27, 1971, when the lady known as the "Bootleg Queen" was laid to rest. Her name was Cleo Epps, and her goodness transcended her law-breaking ways. But unfortunately for her, her cooperation with the right side of the law was what led to her death.

A member of the right side of the law who knew her well was Tulsa's longtime district attorney S.M. "Buddy" Fallis—a man who prosecuted more than seventy jury trials, many of them high profile.

A 1960 graduate of the University of Tulsa Law School (where he later taught), Fallis was well established in his private practice when, in 2011, he spoke with *Voices of Oklahoma* from his office in Tulsa's Old City Hall about the bootlegging legend Cleo Epps.

"She got that name, Queen of the Bootleggers, back during a federal grand jury here in Tulsa County, in which a police commissioner in Tulsa was indicted and some high officials were indicted, and bootleggers were indicted for conspiracy for allowing alcohol to be sold illegally. She was subpoenaed to go before the grand jury, and I remember looking at newspaper articles about this.

"She was standing in the hall waiting, I guess, to go in and testify when her picture was taken, and somebody at one of the papers used as a caption under the picture, 'Cleo Epps, the Bootleg Queen.'

"She was a bootlegger, there was no question about that. But she had, I think, been a schoolteacher at one time. She was a very physically strong person. She had actually physically participated in the building of the houses in an addition where she lived, down almost on the Tulsa County/Creek County line. And she blew stumps out of the ground with dynamite in order to make room for the houses and physically, physically did the labor. She was a physically strong person."

The repeal of Prohibition in Oklahoma in 1959 put her and her fellow bootleggers out of business. (Prior to Prohibition, illegal alcohol would be transported into Oklahoma, and bootleggers, called that for hiding booze in the wearers' boots, would provide distribution service to individual customers' homes.)

In the process of doing business outside of the law, Cleo Epps met some less-than-distinguished citizens, two of whom decided to swing an election. "Apparently, these two yahoos, Albert McDonald and Lester Pugh, thought they were doing a favor to their friend and lawyer.... They thought if they put Judge Fred Nelson out of the race that their friend would probably win. That's cockamamie thinking, but at the same time, these criminal types, they may be sharp in their ways on how to steal and kill, but they're not too sharp sometimes when it comes to reasoning," recalls Fallis.

They blew up the judge's car, but he survived. And during the course of the investigation, Cleo Epps told Fallis that McDonald and Pugh had obtained some dynamite from her—dynamite she had left over from blowing up stumps. Fallis asked, "If there was a grand jury, would you testify?" And she said, "Yes, if I can do it in disguise." That was quite a leap for her, and so Fallis agreed.

"So, anyway, we have the grand jury, and Cleo Epps did testify in disguise. Matter of fact, I had to look at her twice to recognize who she was when they brought her in there."

Buddy Fallis was not the only one who recognized her, though, for later she disappeared and soon was found dead—murdered.

Which resulted in many distinguished mourners at her funeral. But why?

"In my communications with Cleo Epps, she was actually a very soft-spoken woman who seemed truly compassionate toward people. She was generous and had the reputation of helping people in that community. Was she a bootlegger? Yes. She probably would have been the first to say, 'Yeah, I've done that. I've sold whiskey.' But I think that you'd have to look at how black was that crime in view of the times. I mean, again, it was a state that would vote dry and buy wet. So, I'm not apologizing for it. But I'd say that I found her to be a compassionate person and a person that was well liked.

"As a matter of fact, there's a couple, a little couple that testified in these trials that lived in one of her houses. She would have dinner with them just about every night. They were older people. And the husband in that family, he had been helping Cleo because she helped them. He'd been helping her paint a barn on the day that she disappeared. That was a very common practice. You know, come in the back door, sit down at the table, have a meal. And that's when her killer came and got her and took her away on the night she was killed.

"They remembered him coming to the house and being the last person that had seen Cleo alive. But yeah, I think that probably it's sort of like a character out of a Damon Runyon story, you might say. Did she have a negative standpoint from the standpoint of being a bootlegger at one time? I guess. But did she do a lot of good? The people over there apparently thought she did. I think the other thing, too, is law enforcement likes to curry and criminals sometimes like to curry a communication line with them. So that they can tell you things and rest assured that they're not going to be exposed in that. Or who knows, maybe even not tell you things. But she was liked."

For more of Buddy Fallis's stories about growing up in Tulsa, the famous Girl Scout murder trial, and other key cases he prosecuted, go to www.VoicesofOklahoma.com.

It was a little bit after 4:00 coming up on 5:00 when we got the call from the dispatcher that there had been a shooting at Southern Hills.

—MIKE HUFF

George Matson's relationship with a leader in Tulsa's business community went beyond golf shop employee to country club member.

This man, who saved $400 from painting houses in Ireland for passage on the SS *America* to New York City and then by train to Tulsa, and the chairman of Telex Corp. were by any standard good friends.

That friendship was cemented by Matson's ability to schedule an early tee-time at Southern Hills Country Club, recognized as one of the nation's Top 25 golf courses. "Get me an early tee time and join us on the plane," Matson would be told—the plane being a private one from Tulsa to Norman or other venues to see the businessman's favorite football teams. As long as Matson could get someone to fill in for him at the golf shop on game days, he would fly with his pal to OU games—both home and away.

As he recalled for the *Voices of Oklahoma* oral history website in 2015, "Roger Wheeler and I were good friends."

On May 27, 1986, Roger Wheeler was the victim of a gunshot between the eyes in the Southern Hills Country Club parking lot and his good friend, George Matson, was the first person on the scene.

It would be two decades before anyone was indicted for his murder.

"Roger played golf and he came in and changed clothes and so forth. I said, 'Roger, how'd you play?' He said, 'You'd better change my handicap because these people are going to kill me.' I say, 'Oh, Roger, we'll check the handicap.' And sure enough, here it is, he walked out to the car and there was a bang. I went out and wanted to know what was going on. And the kids on the swimming board were pointing to the car.

"I went out and opened the car door and I didn't recognize who it was. And I went around to get the other door open and I couldn't get it open because it was locked. And I went back and fumbled around and got it opened."

By then Matson recognized the victim was the friend he talked with minutes before.

"I turned him around and I was going to give him resuscitation and there was no use, he was gone then. Then I ran in and told them in the golf shop, 'Call the police! And call an ambulance.' And the police came up and I told them what was going on. And I kind of slipped out of the way for awhile. You're nervous and you're worked up. I was trying to calm myself down. I had spoken to him a minute or two earlier, or less. He walked out to his car, and bang."

The first detective on the scene was a 25-year-old who, at the time of Wheeler's murder, was discussing where to go to dinner with his fellow police officers. Mike Huff shared his recollections with the *Voices of Oklahoma* oral history website in 2013.

"I was a little bit frustrated that homicide wasn't as action-packed as I was wanting it to be and I remember I was on evening shift and myself and a couple other guys, we were trying to figure out where we were going to eat dinner. It was the big decision of the night. It was a little bit after 4:00 coming up on 5:00 when we got the call from the dispatcher that there had been a shooting at Southern Hills.

"It's just kind of like on TV. You grab your coat and your radio and you're heading out the door and everybody's got their two cents' worth. So, we were thinking maybe it was the kitchen help or maybe a lawn crew had a dispute or something like this. We weren't really getting any information on it because it was on a different frequency than we were assigned. We all drove out there just as fast as we could in 5:00 traffic and pulled in there and see a Cadillac with the driver slumped over with a bullet wound between the eyes and I'm thinking, 'Wow, this is not the cleanup crew or not the lawn crew.' That's where the twists and turns started that particular day.

"Mr. Wheeler was seated in a late-model Cadillac. He was dressed in a suit. He had a leather workout bag with his golf club in it, and you knew that there was a successful Southern Hills Club member seated behind that wheel and shot between the eyes. Right outside the door were several live rounds of .38-caliber ammunition lying on the ground. A lot of speculation as to what that meant. In fact, years of speculation as to what that meant. It turned out that the murder weapon fell apart when that one fatal bullet was fired—spilling the other ammunition onto the parking lot.

"There was just one bullet fired, which kind of makes you think that somebody knew what they were doing. So, we just had the task of that whole methodical process that night."

Huff's mind jumped to another recent crime in the neighborhood. "I had just a couple of weeks before gotten involved in an investigation where a successful man, just a few blocks away from Southern Hills, got robbed and threatened with a gun about 58th and Harvard. That was my first thought. I'm thinking, you know, maybe they were trying to rob him because he had a very expensive gold watch on that was visible, and maybe something went bad. You know, if I look back when I was 25 years old, I was naïve. I was not worldly, if you will, and you look back to an era that if you don't go to the library and pick up a book to read, that was the sole source of information, and you could only get the three channels on television. Now we're inundated with information. It's so easy to get. A cell phone is a computer. So the thought of the Mafia coming to Tulsa wasn't in my wheelhouse."

Soon, however, suspicion led to speculation that the murder was a mob hit. But when at Huff's request the Tulsa FBI asked the Boston FBI office for help, they received a terse reply that Boston had ruled out a Boston Mafia connection. Thus began years of a relentless pursuit by Mike Huff with resources provided by the Tulsa Police Department, other organizations in Boston, and federal agencies to identify those connected to the murder of Roger Wheeler.

It turned out that one of the key figures who was ultimately indicted for Wheeler's murder was a former FBI agent—in Boston.

For more of Mike Huff's oral history—how he unraveled the Wheeler case, the role the infamous Whitey Bulger played, and the roadblocks Huff had to overcome, as well as its conclusion—go to www.VoicesofOklahoma.com.

The Run for Land
(Some Came by Train)

Long before Woody Guthrie was singing about your land and my land, and before Rodgers and Hammerstein declared in the state song that the land was grand, there was a hole in the map of the United States. Almost smack-dab in its center. Oh, there were signs of early civilizations having spent time on it, and Spanish explorers had crossed it, and French fur traders had ventured into it, but there were no permanent settlers.

Until.

Native Americans, some by choice, others by US government force, began calling it home—home by names they brought with them.

But the westward movement of a so-called manifest destiny also brought pale visages into the hole in the map that was called Indian Territory. Primarily by land runs, this virgin territory was eventually claimed by visionaries, merchants, and ordinary people. Their legacy is found in Oklahomans of today who recall the stories of grit and determination handed down from more than a century ago.

They went from Pittsburg, Kansas, to No Man's Land in a covered wagon with a small herd of cattle.

—HENRY BELLMON

When you look at a map of Indian Territory, it fairly closely resembles the State of Oklahoma—with one exception. What is now known as Oklahoma's Panhandle is not included. Rather, what was to become Oklahoma resembled a rectangle on three sides, with the Red River at its south.

The land that is today's Oklahoma's Panhandle was not included for one simple fact: officially it was called "Public Land Strip." Unofficially it was known as "No Man's Land."

It was upon those high plains of No Man's Land that esteemed Oklahoma statesman Henry Bellmon's family got its first taste of what was to become Oklahoma.

"My dad was a teenager, or still in grade school, when his father, who had been a strip miner in Kansas, moved to what was then no-man's land. It is now known as Beaver County, Oklahoma," recalled the former governor and US senator. Their mode of transportation was common to that era, as "they went from Pittsburg, Kansas, to No Man's Land in a covered wagon with a small herd of cattle. I don't know how many were in that herd, but they went right down the main street in Wichita, which was hardly more than a village at the time."

Bellmon recalled that the new arrivals lived in a dugout on the banks of the Beaver River, also known as the North Canadian River, and made a living "by working for the local ranchers and by hauling buffalo bones that they picked up on the prairie to deliver them and sell and bring merchandise back to the local storekeepers." Home, a dugout, "was on the bank of the river in the ground. They had no other materials to make a house from. There were no trees out there.

"I think there were three kids and their parents, so there were five people living in a dugout," which is another word for a horizontal hole in the ground. At least it gave them some shelter from the wind that would come sweeping down the plains. "My dad talked about driving a team of horses and hauling bones to deliver them in the wind and the wind blew out of the north. He said it was so cold that the only way they could stay alive was to get in behind the horses and walk behind the horses in the doubletree harness for what little protection the horses gave them from the wind."

While the times and temperatures could be grim, all members of the family survived, but not without an occasional unnecessary risk, as Bellmon recalls.

"My dad talked about doing things that were pretty deadly. The prairie rattlesnakes lived with the prairie dogs. My dad and his partner made a game of going into prairie dog towns about sundown and the rattlesnakes were coiled up outside their dens. They would take their lariat ropes and loop them over and make it into a kind of a club. And they killed as many rattlesnakes as they could before the snakes got wise and went down the holes. If they would have made a mistake and gotten bitten, they wouldn't have had any way of getting treated."

After some five years, Bellmon said, "My father's father became tired of pioneering, so they went back to Kansas," but his father would return, only the next time to a more centralized location.

Meanwhile, the maternal side of Bellmon's family was as familiar with covered wagons as his paternal side. "My mother's family worked as farmers up by Clarinda, Iowa. They came here in 1907. I have the accounts from other members of the family telling about the trip, which I think took about three weeks. They came in two covered wagons and they shipped their farming machinery down by train, so it came later.

"They came when the weather was nice, and they made it into kind of a picnic. They had to forge some rivers, and when they did they would go fishing and swimming; they made it into a pleasant experience. My mother was one of the older children, and I think she walked a lot of the distance alongside the wagon from Iowa down to here."

I was talking with Bellmon at what he called "our home place, which is seven miles east and one mile south from Billings, ten miles directly south of Tonkawa, and sixteen miles north and due west of Perry." He calls it "our home place" for good reason. After the family returned to Kansas, Bellmon's father cast his eyes south.

"In 1893 when the Cherokee Strip opened, my father was too young to make the run, but he came down in 1897 and bought another man's rights to his claim and lived on the plain, which is across the road from where we are sitting today."

This "home place" proved to be valuable for the young Henry Bellmon's future. While his mother, Edith, "had a teacher's certificate that allowed her to teach in the country schools, and she taught in the one-room school here in this neighborhood," his father, George Delbert, "was not an educated man." But he believed in education—even for a family of thirteen children, which included nine from a first marriage that ended in the passing of his wife.

"It wasn't easy for my folks to help us with education because during the Depression money was very tight. In fact, except for some lucky breaks, my dad would have had to give up the land and move off. An oil company came here and dug a well and gave my dad enough of the royalties that at least that let him stay on the land."

From that came a strong advocate for education who became not only a US senator, but also Oklahoma's first Republican governor.

For more of Henry Bellmon's oral history—his World War II near-death experience, his decision to enter public service, and his fight on behalf of education funding in Oklahoma, go to www.VoicesofOklahoma.com.

I think it's always been interesting that he made the Land Run on the Santa Fe Railroad.
—WILLIAM J. ROSS

The image of the Oklahoma Land Run of 1889 is of men on horseback, horse-drawn carriages, wagons—anything on wheels that a horse could be attached to—and even a man or two on bicycles making a dusty dash for land. What this image misses, however, is the train—the Santa Fe train that also brought settlers and claim stakers to Indian Territory.

One Oklahoman who knows that part of the Land Run saga well is Oklahoma City's distinguished lawyer William J. "Bill" Ross, who served as an attorney for E.K. Gaylord Sr., publisher of the *Daily Oklahoman,* and who was a recipient of the University of Oklahoma Regents Alumni Award for his extensive involvement with his alma mater (both his undergraduate and law degrees were from OU). He remembers well the Dust Bowl and the Great Depression, as well as stories from family members who staked their claim in Oklahoma soil, in his oral history interview for the *Voices of Oklahoma* website.

"It was at a point north of Purcell right there on the South Canadian River at noon on April 22, 1889," Ross said from the offices of his two foundations—the Inasmuch Foundation, and the Ethics and Excellence in Journalism Foundation—in 2012. "I've heard it was a beautiful, sunny, blue-sky day. The guns went off, and the train and the horses and the carriages and wagons and the people on foot all took off running.

"I think it's always been interesting that my grandfather made the Land Run on the Santa Fe Railroad. The word is that in earlier years a horse stepped on his foot or something. He didn't like horses at all, so he was much happier making the Land Run on the Santa Fe Railroad," said Ross, noting, "I think 12 miles per hour was the fastest the train could go. They tried to calibrate it to the speed of a horse, so it wouldn't have an advantage and beat everyone up here.

"So the train came on up to the station in Oklahoma City, which was a little bit south of where the present Santa Fe station is located. It sounds too good to be true, but I understand that he walked across the street and staked out a lot on the corner of California, which is now E.K. Gaylord's. I don't know what all was involved in staking his claim on that piece of land, but he ended up with it and he started to construct his bakery there."

That was the reason Ross's grandfather was on that Santa Fe train. "My grandfather had a bakery in Gainesville, Texas. The lands were opening up here in Oklahoma. He thought that was a good opportunity, so he made the Land Run into Indian Territory," said Ross. His grandfather, George Ross, who was an orphan, had made his way to Gainesville by way of St. Louis, where he had been raised by an order of nuns. "He had a very good education up through the seventh or eighth grade. He was bilingual. He left school when he was about fourteen years old. It's my understanding that he went to live with a family in the St. Louis area. I don't think that worked out very well, so I think he took off six months or a year after he went to live with them. I don't know anything about the interim."

What Ross *did* know is that George Ross ended up in Gainesville, where he married Justina Westerman, an immigrant from Germany. "My grandmother stayed down in Gainesville, Texas, until the building was completed in the middle of May in 1889. I guess they were married in 1885, because my uncle George was born in late 1886 and my dad was born on June 21, 1888. So my dad was about eleven months old when my grandmother brought him and my uncle George to Oklahoma City on the train.

"They moved into the back of the bakery at first, then later that summer they moved into a hotel or something. Eventually they had a lot down on Washington Street, which is now Second Street. They sold the lot where they had built their house to Oklahoma Gas & Electric in the 1920s.

"After they made the Run and got settled in and everything, my grandfather was on the second city council in Oklahoma City. He was always involved in the affairs of the city and very interested in it apparently. He was on the city council and he spoke English and he spoke French from his early days. He also spoke German, because my grandmother taught him that. My grandmother would not allow German to be uttered in her house once they moved to the United States. This was the Land of Promise, and she was not going to have that. But apparently, she did teach him German when she first got over here. He translated the city charter to be voted on into the other two languages. There was a quite extensive German population here at that time."

The grandfather became a city leader after taking a train to stake his claim in the barren land that would become Oklahoma City, and his grandson would do the family name proud.

For more of Bill Ross's oral history—memories of the city's Dust Bowl days, working as a local delivery boy during World War II, and E.K. Gaylord Sr.—go to www.VoicesofOklahoma.com.

And when you got to the piece of land that you thought was going to be yours, you had to go and pull up the stakes.
—CATHARINE KINGSLEY

To most people, the expression "pulling up stakes" is an announcement that the speaker is leaving. But during the April 22, 1889, Oklahoma Land Run it had a far different meaning, as Catharine Benson Kingsley revealed in her Oklahoma oral history interview on the *Voices of Oklahoma* website in 2010.

A 1943 Oklahoma State University (then Oklahoma A&M) graduate with a language major, Catharine Kingsley mastered five of them—English, Spanish, French, German, and Latin. During World War II, she moved to Washington, DC, to scan intercepted enemy correspondence, looking for repetitive letters and words and patterns that could convey secret messages. The lady from Stillwater was a code breaker. But long before her war service, her grandfather, James H. Kirkpatrick, and grandmother, Ida Grove Kirkpatrick, pulled up stakes in Kansas to *literally* pull up stakes in the unassigned lands that would become Oklahoma.

"It was the Great Land Rush," Kingsley recalled, with her ancestors leaving Douglass, Kansas, for 160 acres "south of Perkins, which would be eleven to thirteen miles south of Stillwater."

While the sound of the gun at noon on that April day in 1889, and the resulting rush for land, is what is most memorable about that date, the details of the day are equally important.

As Kingsley told the *Voices of Oklahoma* oral history website, "The army engineers came and staked out all the land in the 160 acres. And they put stakes on them. And when you got to the piece of land that you thought was going to be yours, you had to go and pull up the stakes. Well, maybe there was somebody else on the other corner so they all had to fight it out. But when a person had the stakes that he needed, he took them to the land grant office that was in Guthrie, which was our first capital.

"After they had lived on the land and produced whatever they could grow, at the end of five years you went back to the land grant office and you showed proof that you had actually improved on the land. And then you got it. You actually earned your 160 acres," said Kingsley, recalling the stories she had been told.

"The land office and the army engineers had done all the work about the stakes and where the 160 acres were. And anybody that wanted the land, then they had to pull up the stakes and have them in their hands when they went to register that that was the farm they got," affirmed Kingsley. Fortunately, there were no disputes over the stakes pulled by James H. Kirkpatrick.

She also recalled a story from another land run. "Over in Enid they had the 1893 Cherokee Strip. Some of the people in that run took their family in the wagon with them, you know. And they pulled the wagon with the children in it. This one little girl fell off, so they just left her there on that piece of land 'cause they knew the better land was further on.

"Well, when they got there all the stakes were pulled up, so they had to go back and get their little girl. When they got back to her, they found that the stakes were still there in the ground, so they pulled them up and that's what they took.

"In later years, it is one of the most oil-producing farms around Enid anywhere. They're a wealthy family now 'cause they went back to the land nobody wanted where their little girl had fallen out of the wagon."

Kingsley's grandfather's land was not as fortunate. "My grandfather didn't have that luck. We didn't get an oil-producing farm." Her grandfather had to work.

After pulling the stakes and claiming his land, Kirkpatrick "went back to Douglass, you know, to get his family. And he brought them down and he had three daughters. They lived on that land.

"They had sort of a log house he built, and when I was a girl we went down, and I saw the house they lived in. He was a drayman; a dray is a wagon that is pulled by a horse or horses. And he made scheduled trips to Kansas to go get flour and sugar because they didn't have that down here, and there weren't grocery stores very much. He did that, and he helped people move their furniture and different things. He was kind of like what we call a moving van now.

"But he went periodically to bring back things that they needed that they didn't have in the stores in Perkins or Stillwater.

And then when they later moved to Stillwater, he was still a dray-man there for the city of Stillwater.

"And my grandmother taught at the eighth-grade school. She also helped with all the things on the farm that a wife would do then. They had hens. They kept the eggs and she took them to Perkins to a little store to sell them. And she rode on horse-back sidesaddle. It was about five or six miles. She had to ford the Cimarron River to get there. She had nine dozen eggs and they sold for three cents a dozen."

And it all started by pulling up stakes.

For more of Catharine Kingsley's oral history—how she coped with the Great Depression, the impact of the attack on Pearl Harbor on the Oklahoma A&M campus, and the letter she received from J. Edgar Hoover, go to www.VoicesofOklahoma.com.

But, oh my, the pageant system is so wonderful for shy girls.

—JANE JAYROE GAMBLE

As difficult as it is to imagine, Oklahoma's Jane Jayroe Gamble, Miss America of 1967, television anchor, author, and public official, is shy.

"When I was a freshman in high school, the summer before my freshman year, we moved to Laverne, and that was huge for me. I thought my world would always be in Sentinel, where life was very secure and small. Then we moved, and I freaked out.

"I can remember the first day of school, it was the first day my mother was teaching school and she took me to school and I wouldn't get out of the car. She was like, 'I have to be at work. This is my first day too. You have to get out of the car.' And I wouldn't get out. But I did, and I met a few of the kids and I already had a crush on a boy, so I walked in behind him with all of my books and I tripped and spilled all of my books. I was so humiliated."

One place where she could hide her shyness was on the stage because "inside the shy girl was a performer with dreams." And as Miss America she no longer had to introduce herself to people, for when she walked in a room everyone knew who she was.

Yet, to this day, shyness is an issue with this poised and accomplished woman.

"There are parts of your personality that you can't really change. And I've accepted that. You learn skills to deal with that. I have to push myself in new circumstances, new social circumstances. But, oh my, the pageant system is so wonderful for shy girls."

World War II

W orld wars are fought on many fronts. World War II was no different.

Oklahomans, and people who would later in life call Oklahoma home, fought on the battlefield, served in Washington, DC, suffered under the Nazis, and fought and were captured by the enemy. They came out as more than survivors, because each one (three men and one woman) served with honor, in his or her own unique way.

There were around three thousand Japanese on the Marshall Islands, and they know we are coming.

—REX CALVERT

As a member of the Fourth Marine Division, Rex Calvert fought in four battles and earned the Purple Heart during World War II. At the age of eighty-eight, he told the *Voices of Oklahoma* oral history website about the day that caused the world of a Central High School senior to dramatically change.

"I was a senior in high school, and I was at Third and Main. In those days they put out an extra paper. These boys would stand on the street and yell, 'Extra! Extra!' The Japanese had bombed Pearl Harbor. We said to each other, 'Where in the world is Pearl Harbor?' Boy, did we ever find out.

"I had no idea what that meant. Teachers did not seem to want to talk about it. A lot of the boys wanted to enlist right away, and some of them did. Some of the boys were only sixteen, and they had to get their parents' permission to join the service. I wanted to stay in school. What does a kid who is nineteen know about what's going on in the world—I mean, what's war? We weren't trained to know anything about that."

Calvert graduated and went to work for Mid-Continent Petroleum. "I worked in their laboratory testing oil because in high school I was my chemistry teacher's assistant. That was quite a big deal for me. I loved to figure out how things worked. I once made hydrogen, the lightest known gas, and put it into a balloon. I signed my name to it and I cast it off, but I didn't hear anything back about who found the balloon. I worked in that laboratory for about ten months before I got my letter and I was told to report to a place and that night I was gone.

"There was army, navy, and the marines, and they said, 'Which one do you want? You can be in any one, which one do you want to be?' I said, 'I sure like that blue uniform.' So they suckered me into the marine corps, and I was on my way. They said, 'There are no trains leaving Tulsa for San Diego, they all leave from OKC.' So I had to catch a bus and go down there. They said, 'You can have a Pullman car, and they will feed you and take you to San Diego.'

"I got to OKC and they said, 'They gave you the wrong information, there's no Pullman car for you.' I think that recruit man pocketed the money and gave me a coach car that didn't have any seats. It was full of people going to the West Coast to see their husbands in the service. There were women in there with babies crying and vomiting and sour milk smell. There were dirty diapers on the floor. I had to stand up all the way to San Diego—two days and a night. The train stopped every mile or so to pick up a can of milk. You could not get the windows up. There was no air-conditioning on the train and no place to sit down, and all of these people in there. I hate to tell this kind of a story, but these are true facts."

Calvert was soon seeing much different action.

"The first operation we had was in the Marshall Islands. These marines had never killed anybody, and they had never been shot at. They schooled us a little bit. We had some lieutenants that were college educated at the officer's training school on the East Coast. They thought they were hot stuff. They told us, 'Tomorrow morning we are going to land in the Marshall Islands, which is a bunch of coral sticking up out of the ocean. The pieces that are sticking up are just little pieces of land that have accumulated over millions of years. It might be as big as a football field. If it has Japanese gunners on it, we've got to go in and take it.'

"The navy was going to bombard these islands for several days before we got there. They had a little plaster-of-paris model with the beaches numbered and everything. It showed where some of the guns were and where some of the blockhouses were. We were supposed to memorize that, and the next day at 2:30 a.m. they were going to wake us up and tell us to get our gear on, issue us ammunition, and we were to land on those two little islands.

"There were around three thousand Japanese on it, and they know we are coming. Some of them were in blockhouses, and some of them were in spider-traps. A spider-trap is just a hole with a cover over it that looks like grass. They could raise that cover up, and if you walked by it, they've got you. They were up in the trees too. We tried to cut all the trees down. If you look at the pictures, they were coconut trees, but shellfire cut those trees down and there were lot of coconuts in the water. We would shoot into the coconut trees because they were killing us. A guy would fall out of the tree and hit the ground, and we would put another shell into him. We were learning how to kill.

"At 2:30 a.m., they said, 'Get your gear on and we will meet in about fifteen minutes down at the galley.' There were no chairs, so we all stood. They had trays and you went by that bunch of hogwash (food) that they had there for you. We were supposed to have steak and eggs and orange juice. Guess what? We got down there and it was the same old story. These were navy people and they don't like marines anyway. They said, 'Well, we ran out of steak, but we've got these wieners and we've got beans and we've got oranges.' We would break open the oranges that had been in a crate with the navy stacking stuff on them. They were bruised and not fit to eat, really, but we would grab two or three of them and put them in our pack so the next day when we didn't have anything to eat, we would have them.

"They wanted us to go down these rope ladders. That rope ladder was nothing but a cargo net that we used to climb from the ship to a smaller boat. So we were getting ready to go down the rope ladder. There was a preacher standing there. One of the boys said to him, 'Father, could you say a prayer for us? Some of us in the next few minutes are going to be casualties.' So he laid his hands on one of the boy's heads and said a little prayer to the Man Upstairs. We were getting ready to climb down, and we saw the Father with a .45. We said, 'Excuse me, sir, but if you are a man of the cloth, why are you putting that .45 on?' He said, 'Well, boys, I will tell you. Prayer is good, but this is faster.'"

For more of Rex Calvert's oral history—going over the side of the ship, the anti-tank gun that could shoot three hundred steel balls, and his two other landings— go to www.VoicesofOklahoma.com.

There were no lights on any of the buildings in the district. They thought the Germans would come to bomb Washington, DC

—CATHARINE KINGSLEY

It wasn't enough for Catharine Kingsley to come from a pioneer family. She was a pioneer herself in responding when her country called during World War II—working as a code breaker for the Federal Bureau of Investigation.

She recalled her days during the war in the nation's capital for the *Voices of Oklahoma* website in 2010.

Following graduation from Oklahoma A&M in 1943 as a language major, fluent in Spanish and French, Kingsley received a scholarship to the University of Colorado. "I wasn't very happy really at Boulder. I'd never been that far away from my family, so I didn't go very long. When I had a chance to come home, I did. So, I went up to the offices at A&M that had the foreign languages to ask them things, and they told me that the FBI was looking for people who could be good translators and do cryptanalysis. So I applied."

On August 31, 1944, she received a letter from J. Edgar Hoover that read: "Dear Ms. Benson (her maiden name): You are hereby offered an appointment in the Federal Bureau of Investigation, United States Department of Justice, as a laboratory technician in grade SP5 with salary at the rate of $1,800 per annum." (After deductions, that came out to less than $200 a month. That, however, was not a concern for Kingsley: "I'd lived through the Depression, I had money enough to do what I wanted. And then they came in and they wanted you to buy war bonds. So I bought a lot of war bonds. I put a lot of my money in war bonds 'cause I didn't need it. I think my room where I was, and I lived in a barracks, was like twelve dollars per month.")

The letter concluded: "Advise by wire collect of your acceptance or declination of this appointment. If you do not report for duty by the aforementioned date, the appointment will be canceled. Sincerely, John Edgar Hoover, Director."

Kingsley reported for duty.

"We didn't go by airplane, we went by train. There was another Stillwater girl, she had been offered a job with the State Department. So we rode the train together and we lived in the same barracks, but she worked one place and I worked the other. On weekends we could do things together, but a lot of times at the FBI if there were things that we were needing to do they had to know where we were. In case an emergency came up they'd call us back on Sunday.

"There were no lights on any of the buildings in the district. They thought the Germans would come to bomb Washington, DC. We had blackout curtains so that if we had lights on they would be all closed, even if we worked late at night. All messages that we got came by telegraph or radio, and sometimes over the phone. They were stamped the date they arrived and the time they arrived. And we had twenty-four hours to do what we had to do to either try to break the code or to decipher a code that had been broken. And so, if the message was supposed to have gone to the army or the navy or the marines, the State Department, or the OSS (the forerunner of the CIA), we would pass it on. Congress had mandated things that the FBI would do, which was more security for the United States. And we didn't do any of the codes for the armed services."

First order of business for a new code-breaker was to study how to break codes. "Well, you see some of these books [pointing to nearby volumes], these are the ones we studied. So we learned what they said, what the codes were like. And then there are books that the FBI had that were classified and you couldn't take them home. You just studied them at work. So then when a code came that we hadn't been able to break, well then, some of us worked on them. And we had to decide which particular code that they used.

"The ones that were really harder to break I expect were the German ones. The Germans are not anything but intelligent. But the Japanese were easier broken because their written language is all those little brush things with the ink. And they had to turn all those into telegraphic like our Arabic alphabet is. So they were easier broken. But if we got a lot of codes that came from about the same place, and we thought that was so, well then, they could be superimposed. And you could kind of figure out, 'Well, here's this.' And sometimes there would be a little blank space, sometimes if they came by telegraph it was garbled so that made it hard to even decipher if the code had been broken."

Learning the language was important, for words had to fit "just like when you do crossword puzzles, they give you a clue and you see, well, there's only five spaces or ten spaces, whatever it is, and you have to find a word that fits in there. Well, it's the same way, you have to understand the language well enough to know which words come first and in the middle and whatever."

And then she met the man who had signed her hiring letter.

"When we had finished our cryptanalysis studies and everything and then we were actually working on the codes and deciphering everything, we all had a nice reception and J. Edgar Hoover shook our hands. And I've never had such a good handshake in my life. He was a real strong man. He'd congratulate us all and he talked to us and that's how I met him. It was graduation from my studies. I liked him real well. Everybody liked him. In later years they say things about him I wonder if it's true, but it wasn't true in wartime."

For more of Catharine Kingsley's oral history—her Dust Bowl days, more about the secrets of code-breaking, and life in wartime DC, go to www.VoicesofOklahoma.com.

I had long braids. One woman grabbed my hair and cut them off, and the next one shaved my head.

—EVA UNTERMAN

On October 12, 2010, Eva Unterman was speaking with the *Voices of Oklahoma* website from her home in Garden Park in Tulsa. She paused to describe the day. "I am looking out the window here and the sun is shining, and I'm looking at a beautiful blue morning glory. I am enjoying that view very much."

Many people would consider it a miracle that Eva Unterman could enjoy that fall day in 2010. For in the summer of 1939, she was a little girl in Lodz, Poland, who was looking forward to the first grade. While on the family's summer vacation, she heard her family quietly talking about Germany and war. They cut short their vacation and went home to Lodz, and soon little Eva was looking at black, shiny boots as she was forced onto a train. The German invasion of Poland was underway.

"We were made to get out of the train, and I do remember these people, SS, standing there and screaming at us in German, yelling for us to get out quickly and using their whips. Men and women were immediately separated. I no longer saw my father, but I stayed with my mother and my grandmother. We were made to go to the right, where a selection took place. I didn't know what it meant, but the younger, healthier-looking women went to one side, and the older, the sick, and the children to the other. We had no idea why. This was done very efficiently and quickly. We left all our belongings in the train, and we were told that we would get them later. We were made to run toward the right side, Mother holding on to my hand, and we came to this large building that I believe it was made of concrete. We were made to go inside, where long tables were set up where SS women were sitting there, who were every bit as brutal as the men, and they were processing us.

"The SS were our guards; an elite unit of people who volunteered for it. They were there in all of the concentration death camps and various labor camps. It certainly was better for them to be in charge of these poor Jews than to go to the east and fight.

"Next, we had to take all of our clothes off. I had long braids. One woman grabbed my hair and cut them off, and the next one shaved my head. And that was done to all of the women and the few children who were in our group. Then we were led to another building where there were showerheads overhead. We did not know how fortunate we were that water came down on us. After that, as we came out of there, we were given these coarse, dry pajama-like uniforms and wooden shoes and made to go into a certain direction. Well, I know now, which meant nothing to us then, that we were in Auschwitz, a death camp, as it is now known.

"We were there shivering, running toward these barracks. People who visit there now, I have not been there and have no intention of visiting, see that there are still barracks as far as the eye can see. We were taken into one and made to spend the night sitting there on the floor. The next morning, we were marched outside and made to stand to be counted. That was the routine in all of the camps. We were counted and then given a rusty bowl that we were to keep. That is what our daily ration of food was poured in. It consisted of water, turnips, and potato peels. No spoons, mind you. We were not considered human. Animals don't use spoons. And my mother made me drink every bit of that stuff, and you know, we learned to just eat it like that, directly holding the bowl to our mouth and eating it that way. And we got a dry piece of bread that people ate. We were very hungry at that point.

"I should mention that as we, our fortunate group, went to the showers, there was a building that was built to the same specifications where the old, the sick, and the children were taken, and instead of water, poisonous gas descended on them. They were killed, and then their bodies burned in the crematorium ovens built for that purpose.

"So, you see, there were people running this entire machine, this industry of killing. There were people who were building the ovens, who were maintaining them, who produced Zyklon B. It was a business of killing people. There have been many tragedies in human history. And to this day people are being killed for various unbelievable reasons, innocent people, as we speak. But there have never been death factories set up that were so well organized as these.

"Later we were taken to a concentration camp called Stutthof. I don't always tell this story, but I will for this interview. It was every bit as awful as Auschwitz but less well known. And it was in Stutthof that one of the worst memories occurred. We were sitting on the floor in one of the barracks. They were all built to the same specifications, long, low buildings divided lengthwise into three sections. The center section was where mostly SS women would march up and down and beat us and scream at us. Then, there were on both sides these bunks that really were shells. You have probably seen them in a documentary film. Well, that one evening my mother and I sat on the floor in front of those bunks with other women, and my grandmother, Kafeman, sat across on the other side with other women. We were already undernourished and not doing well physically, when from the left side I remember here come the black boots. And they were spiffy looking, clean looking, with starched uniforms, some young men, I believe that one of them was an officer, maybe they all were. And he announced that he was looking for some volunteers to mend their socks for an extra piece of bread.

"I believe that to this day, when my grandmother's hand went up, she was one of the first to volunteer—it was because she wanted to give this piece of bread to me. My mother later told me as she held on to my hand that she wanted to shout to her mother, 'Don't,' but she couldn't, because that would have brought attention to me and I wasn't supposed to be there. As the women were led outside, one of the young men came back laughing. He was laughing. There was no mending to be done. This was Saturday night, and these men entertained themselves by taking these women outside and killing them."

For more of Eva Unterman's oral history—anti-Semitism and survival—go to www.VoicesofOklahoma.com.

Flossenbürg: That was a plain murder camp.
—MARIAN OPALA

Future Oklahoma Supreme Court Justice Marian P. Opala was born January 20, 1921, in Lodz, Poland. In 1939, he had just enrolled in law school when Nazi Germany invaded his homeland. He joined the Polish Army. After Poland's defeat, Opala joined the Polish underground and was eventually taken prisoner in 1944. He shared his World War II experiences with the

Voices of Oklahoma website in October 2010 from the conference room of the Oklahoma Supreme Court in Oklahoma City.

"I was with a group of the AK. *AK* means Home Army people, AK fighters. That probably saved our lives. Because they did not kill us, they did not shoot us, they took us to their headquarters and kept us as persons in a POW (prisoner-of-war) status. All Home Army personnel, by order of the army, were treated as POWs and not as guerillas. We still don't know what prompted the Germans to do that and why Hitler did not resist, because we expected Hitler and the SS to treat us as rebels, as guerillas. So everybody captured in a uniform or wearing insignias of military status, as all of the Polish fighters did, were treated as POWs."

John: You were held in Flossenbürg, a concentration camp in Bavaria?

Marian: That was a plain murder camp.

John: Murder camp?

Marian: Genocide, yes, lots of people died there. It was kind of between a penal concentration camp and true genocide. They worked you to death. They didn't put you into gas chambers, they had no gas chambers, but they worked you to death.

John: That was both Jews and Poles?

Marian: Jews were a small segment. Most people were non-Jewish prisoners from all over Europe: French, Czech, and Dutch—all kinds of people. So I was extremely fortunate to get out of there.

John: Because if they knew who you really were—you were posing as a British soldier, but didn't your accent give you away?

Marian: I did not emphasize my Polishness, that's all I concealed. And they spoke to me in English.

John: So when you spoke English you had an accent, but it didn't dawn on them to think that you were Polish?

Marian: Exactly.

The POWs at the concentration camp where Opala was being held were liberated by the US Army in 1945. "The Germans knew the Russians were coming. They did not want to fall into the hands of the Russian Army. So they started marching all of us westward. They didn't want to be caught guarding us because that might be associated with some cruelties and maybe trials. They abandoned us at night. This happened in Sudetenland. We woke up and there was no one guarding us. It took us quite a while to determine that the guards were gone. And at that point at least the Poles and the Brits were together. Our commanding officer was a British colonel who was smart. He said, 'Hide in haystacks.' He spotted some haystacks, and he hid all of us in haystacks. And the first time we heard American English spoken, the decision had to be made whether and at what time we should identify ourselves and come out. The British colonel orchestrated that. So he waited until those voices could be heard nearby and answered them in British English that 'here we are Polish and British POWs,' and we came out.

"We came out with our hands up because we didn't know what they would do. The Germans were tricky. At times they would pose as Allied soldiers. The British colonel warned us. He said, 'Come out with your arms up.' And I had to translate that into Polish because the British colonel was afraid that some of us would not have our arms up and that they might shoot. And he did it so adroitly. He was afraid that the others wouldn't understand him, so we made sure we came out with our hands up. He didn't want to sacrifice a single life. And he was concerned, which is good military training."

John: Little did he know that he was preserving a future Oklahoma Supreme Court justice.

For more of Marian Opala's oral history—serving as a translator for US forces in occupied Germany and later emigrating to the United States to avoid communist rule, confusion regarding his name of Marian, earning a law degree, and his appointment to the Oklahoma State Supreme Court, go to www.VoicesofOklahoma.com.

A Pulitzer, a Painting, and a Stiletto, Not a Meat Axe

One writer is best known for his Pulitzer Prize for fiction, a painter known for his rendition of one of the most famous field goals in University of Oklahoma football history, and another writer for an editorial that cost his newspaper subscribers. Yet each of these talented Oklahomans accomplished much more during their careers. The Pulitzer Prize winner sparked an interest in American Indian literature, the painter of Uwe von Schamann's field goal was also a noted sculptor, and the editorial writer was the crusading editor of a monthly publication.

But their stories about their famous moments provide details into *how* their influence came about, *why* it happened, and in the case of the editorial that prompted subscription cancellations—the lesson learned.

> *I have expressed the idea, my conviction,*
> *that there is only one story in the world.*
> **—N. SCOTT MOMADAY**

In biblical terms, Native American literature can be divided into two eras: BN, Before N. Scott Momaday; and AN, After N. Scott Momaday. For prior to the publication of his 1969 Pulitzer Prize–winning novel, *House Made of Dawn*, only six Indian authors had published a total of nine novels. By the early 1990s, more than thirty Indians had published novels.

Born in Lawton, Oklahoma, Momaday moved among reservation schools with his parents, who were teachers. Enrolled in the Kiowa Tribe of Oklahoma, he also has received a Cherokee heritage from his mother. He takes justifiable pride in sparking interest in American Indian literature in an oral history conversation with the *Voices of Oklahoma* website in 2010.

"I do feel good about being a part of that movement. I think there are two books that were very influential in bringing to light the possibility of an American Indian Literature. One was *House Made of Dawn* and the other was *Bury My Heart at Wounded Knee*, which was a wonderful history of a thirty-year period in American history. They were both successful and I think made a difference. They convinced the publishing world that here is something being overlooked."

Momaday's next book combined stories he published prior to *House Made of Dawn*.

"*The Way to Rainy Mountain* is simply an elongation of *The Journey of Tai-me*, which was done at the University of California–Santa Barbara, and it was a research project. Three of us made that book, my two colleagues, one being an art professor who specialized in etchings. He made a series of etchings for *The Journey of Tai-me*, and the other partner was a typographer who designed a typeface.

"We gathered the materials and printed the book on our own Washington handpress from the university art department. That became a collector's item. We printed 100 copies and divided them three ways, and most of them have ended up in collections and libraries. That was the prototype of *The Way to Rainy Mountain*. I added commentaries to those stories, and my father illustrated *The Way to Rainy Mountain*. He was such a good artist. Those are all pen-and-ink drawings; they add a very important dimension to the book. Now there's a new edition of it through the University of New Mexico Press."

Using material from *The Journey of Tai-me* was a natural process to Momaday.

"I have expressed the idea, my conviction, that there is only one story in the world. There are many stories *in* the one, but we all take part in that one story. We have our part to play, and so it seems perfectly natural to me that we retell stories and they work in different contexts and they shed light upon different situations, but they are all part of the same thing."

The Way to Rainy Mountain includes fragments of poems, essays, and myths.

"These are all stories. Commentaries, of course, are a different dimension. But the structure of *The Way to Rainy Mountain* is something that I am proud of. Because I discovered that by going from myth, that is, the original oral tale, into history, which is a commentary, then into memoir, which is the personal reminiscence, those are the three voices that inform *The Way to Rainy Mountain*, and they constitute a wheel that seems to me is organic and indispensable to storytelling. That rotation is a never-ending wheel, and I think that's a wonderful thing to work with.

Momaday's autobiography, *The Names: A Memoir*, was published in 1976. He explained the meaning of the title during his oral history conversation with *Voices of Oklahoma* from his condominium in Santa Fe, New Mexico.

"Names and naming are so important in Indian tradition. Names are like flags and coats of arms, identities. People have to live up to their names, and that can sometimes be a very strong challenge. To name something is to confer being on it. So, if you think about it in that sense, you see how important the name-giving ceremony is.

"My Indian name is *Tsoai-talee*, 'rock tree boy.' There is a story about Devil's Tower, Wyoming, which the Kiowas called *Tsoai*, meaning 'rock tree.' I was taken there when I was an infant. It's a very important, sacred place to the Kiowas. So when I returned to Oklahoma with my parents, a man in the tribe came and gave me the name 'rock tree boy' to commemorate my having been taken to this place.

"The story about Tsoai involves a boy who turns into a bear. I have always identified with that boy, and I have bear power, so it's very important to me. I identify with the bear, and I have ties with the bear. The bear is somehow in my disposition and my makeup. It's the most important totem in my life. That's not unusual for Indian people, but the story of the bear and the boy who turns into the bear is very meaningful to me."

In the years following earning a PhD from Stanford University in 1963, Momaday taught at the University of Santa Barbara, University of California's Berkeley campus, Stanford, and the University of Arizona, and he was a visiting professor at Columbia and Princeton Universities, while also being the first professor to teach American Literature in Moscow, Russia, at Moscow State University.

But to book lovers, he is best known as an author, and as with any serious author, readers look for meaning in, well, nearly every word and phrase—a practice that amuses Momaday.

"You write a book and then you put it behind you, and people ask you questions about it and you sometimes have a hard time remembering. It's funny how that happens, and I have fun with it sometimes. People come up to me sometimes and say, 'Dr. Momaday, here in *The Names* on page 142, you wrote this, and did you mean to be ironic or is this a symbol?' You know, I think about for a little bit and then I say, 'Of course. How can you doubt it?'"

For more of N. Scott Momaday's oral history—his youth in Gallop, New Mexico, meeting William Faulkner, and his advice to writers, go to www.VoicesofOklahoma.com.

Switzer called a time-out, called old Uwe over, and he said, "Son, this is for all the marbles."
—JAY O'MEILIA

It was another one of the "games of the century" that seemed to be annual affairs during the 1970s. And this one, the first meeting between two traditional football powers, was living up to every expectation.

September 24, 1977. Columbus, Ohio. Home of the Big Ten's Ohio State University under coaching legend Woody Hayes. The opponent, the Big Eight's University of Oklahoma, under the brash and bold Barry Switzer.

OU dominated early in the game, but the Buckeyes fought back to lead 28 to 26. But in the final minutes, OU had the ball, and with Dean Blevins at quarterback, drove down the field to the Ohio State 37-yard line. Six seconds remained on the clock. Time was called. OU's kicker Uwe von Schamann trotted onto the field.

Present at that moment was Jay O'Meilia, native Oklahoman and noted artist whose works have been displayed in such notable places as the Smithsonian Institution, the National Academy of Design in New York, and the National Cowboy & Western Heritage Museum in Oklahoma City. He was also well known as one of the country's finest sports artists. It was the right time for the right moment for the right artist.

"Switzer called a time-out, called old Uwe over, and he said, 'Son, this is for all the marbles.' Uwe says, 'Don't worry about it, Coach,'" recalled O'Meilia for the *Voices of Oklahoma* oral history website. "Switzer said, 'Uwe, you know normally we kick seven yards back from center. Would it bother you if I tell Mark Lucky,' who was the deep snapper, 'to move it back an extra yard and you kick eight yards back instead of seven?' Uwe said, 'Coach, I don't care if you move it back twelve yards. I am ready to do it.' They moved the spot to place the ball back one extra yard."

After the teams lined up, Ohio State's Hayes called a time-out "and tried to freeze Uwe. That's when Uwe started directing the chants, called out, 'Defense, defense, blah, blah, blah!' And there's Uwe standing there in the middle of the field directing the ensemble. He was cool under fire. And it was at Columbus."

The ball was snapped, spotted, and "when it left his foot,

hell, it was still going. It could have been fifty or sixty yards. It cleared, and it went way up into the stands."

Pandemonium ensued.

Once the field was cleared, Ohio State had three seconds for one play. Their quarterback could not find an open receiver and was downed by the Sooner defense. Game over.

O'Meilia joined the cheering and then went to work. "I had the sketch within a half hour. I'd already sketched it out, called Switzer later because they did kicking assignments on Thursday afternoon, it was always in the afternoon, and I asked Coach if I could come in and, 'Would you set up the blocking assignments the same it was at the game?' He said, 'Why?' I said, 'I want to do a painting of it.'

"'Yeah, okay, O'Meilia, all right, okay.' So they set up, and Uwe went through his motions and they had the same set, and OU players portrayed the Ohio State players, and pretty much re-created the whole scene for me."

After his painting was finished, O'Meilia knew it had commercial possibilities as a print. And he was right. At the unveiling of the painting, sales orders were taken.

"And my poor wife, Jodie, I said, 'Now, here are these order blanks, honey. Now, see if people might want to order them.' So, we had the big unveiling, Uwe was there, Barry was there. And these people started lining up in front of poor Jodie, at five hundred bucks a pop. Some of them were writing checks for five hundred. Credit cards for five hundred. And she was writing these down. I think we had a hundred orders that night at five hundred bucks a pop."

O'Meilia's backers, who financed the making of the prints, made a profit—"they got a percentage, the schools got a percentage,

I got a percentage." And after the fourteen-color handmade seri-graphs were distributed, a memory went up in dens, living rooms, and offices throughout Oklahoma.

But from a historic standpoint, O'Meilia noted one certain detail that made his famous painting/print possible. That little extra yard from the line of scrimmage.

"This kid from Ohio State broke through right after the ball was snapped. He just barely missed blocking the kick. He hit the ground and sprained both of his wrists because he got around there, and he was just determined to block that thing. If it had still been at seven yards, he would have. And he just barely missed that. I mean, that's how great Switzer was as a coach. I mean, he anticipated and asked, 'Would it bother you if we moved it back an extra yard?' The rest is history, you know."

For more of Jay O'Meilia's oral history—his early difficulty in school because he was always drawing pictures, turning down an art scholarship to Yale, and his successful turn to sculpture, go to www.VoicesofOklahoma.com.

———

I remember the headline I put on the editorial about George Wallace: "Armies of the Night." And I ripped him.
—FROSTY TROY

A ward-winning journalist, editor, and publisher Frosty Troy came by writing by reading. And a fire that burned down the Troys' home in McAlester had a lot to do with that.

Well-known for his fourteen years with Tulsa's afternoon newspaper, the *Tribune*, where he was the Washington correspondent, and where as an editorial writer he once cost the newspaper hundreds of subscribers, Troy is even better known as the longtime publisher and editor of the *Oklahoma Observer*. From that post, he lived out the monthly newspaper's motto: to comfort the afflicted and to afflict the comfortable. He was also an acclaimed speaker on three favorite topics: free enterprise, public schools, and politics. But writing was his true forte, and that direction was set by his early reading habits.

After the family home in McAlester fell to fire, the Troys were dispersed for a time. "I lived for two years with Rose Troy, Grandmother Troy. She was a work of art. She had a library, oh my Lord, all the great books of the Western world. And I read them all because I lived with her for two years and there wasn't anything else to do except helping her with her strawberry patch and mowing the lawn. And that was a push mower.

"I've always been a reader. I read everything at Grandmother Troy's. Dad took a couple of magazines, including the Knights of Columbus magazine. And I always read that. I don't know why, but I was just a reader, and I was probably—the plain truth is, as the years went by, I went out for basketball. I was too short. Went out for baseball, and I couldn't hit. My dad managed the Golden Gloves for twenty-two years, and he stopped my first fight because I wouldn't hit the boy back.

"So there wasn't anything else to do but read. And so—by the way, the library was my home away from home. On the way home from school, I would stop at the library. I read all the series of books and so forth. And one day I brought a book up and the librarian said, 'Not yet, Frosty, not yet.'

"It was an art book of nudes. And I was really curious about that."

Troy spoke to the *Voices of Oklahoma*'s oral history website from his *Oklahoma Observer* office in 2011, explaining that his love for reading led to his writing as the junior high reporter for the school newspaper. Later, while serving in Korea, he sent columns back to the hometown newspaper and was threatened with a court martial unless he started having his prose vetted through army headquarters.

After only two semesters at Oklahoma University, Troy accepted a position as a City Hall reporter with the *Tulsa Tribune*—after the dean of the OU journalism school noted how bored Troy was with college.

Eventually Troy became the *Tribune*'s Washington correspondent, and then there was an airport meeting with *Tribune* editor Jenkin Lloyd Jones.

"Jenkin Lloyd Jones was elected president of the US Chamber of Commerce. I was in Washington, and he wanted me to meet him at National Airport, now named Reagan Airport. So I met his flight. He said, 'Come over and sit down. Vic Barnett is going to retire,' and he said that I was going to be the new number-two man. Associate editor, number two. I didn't want the position, but I had no decision to make. He said, 'You're it.' So I went back to Tulsa, private office, secretary. Oh my God, I thought I'd died and gone to heaven. Tripled my salary, whoa, wow."

And then there was a heartfelt editorial and an important lesson in opinion writing.

Alabama's staunch symbol of segregation, George Wallace,

was running for president and coming to a rally at Tulsa's Civic Center. Troy responded.

"I remember the headline I put on the editorial: 'Armies of the Night.' And I ripped him. And Jenkin came back from Washington, called me in. I knew I was going to be fired because we'd lost several hundred subscribers. And I said, 'Oh, I'm so sorry.' And he said, 'Frosty, you remember what I told you writing editorials? A stiletto, never a meat axe.' That's what he said. 'If you don't want to make personal enemies, you'll use a stiletto.' In other words, issues, issues. But I called George Wallace everything but, and guess what?

"As God is my witness. Several years later I was speaking to the Alabama Education Association in Birmingham, and I was on the stage behind the curtain. And I looked out and they had a ramp built back to the podium. And I said, 'What's that for? That's going to get in the way.' And he said, 'No, no, we have a special guest.' And they wheeled George Wallace up, and he apologized. He apologized.

"He said, 'I'm so sorry. You know, I used the N word and I did all these things because I thought, you know, I could carry the southern states and maybe pick up a northern state or two. But I never felt that in my heart.' That's what he said, 'I never felt that in my heart.' And let me tell you, there wasn't a dry eye in the house. And it was 80 percent black because you know where the whites have gone? Private schools. Wow.

"That's one of my great memories. I didn't speak with him. I shook his hand when he came in, but I wouldn't dare. You know, I'm not that brave. If he and I are in heaven together, I want to apologize because it was a meat axe. I attacked him personally. And that's the wrong way to go.

"And by the way, in fourteen years on the *Tulsa Tribune* I never was ordered to slant a story. And I never slanted a story. And that's a miracle, let me tell you."

For more of Frosty Troy's oral history—his "near miss" at becoming an Eagle Scout, losing two brothers to war, and running the Oklahoma Observer, go to www.VoicesofOklahoma.com.

Breaking the Glass Ceiling

Four women who would not settle for the status quo. Four women who demonstrated perseverance, dedication, and knowledge to become leaders in a world that had built barriers to people such as they are. Barriers built simply because they were women. But the barriers (collectively known as the "glass ceiling") proved to be but temporary impediments along the way to positions of power, influence, and leadership.

Wilma Mankiller, Nancy Feldman, Norma Eagleton, Penny Williams. We are not likely to see their kind again—not because there are no women today with similar perseverance, dedication, and knowledge, but because Mankiller, Feldman, Eagleton, and Williams broke the glass ceiling in their respective fields for others to pass through.

I think that they eventually began to see that I meant what I said.

—WILMA MANKILLER

Wilma Mankiller became the first female principal chief of the Cherokee Nation when its chief, Ross Swimmer, accepted a position with President Ronald Reagan's administration—she was deputy chief and moved up to chief. It was a shock. Almost as big a shock as when Ross Swimmer asked her to run as his deputy chief running mate.

That was many years removed from growing up at Mankiller Flats "in rural Adair County, about twenty miles from Tahlequah, about fifteen miles from Stilwell. When I was a kid, there was no paved road near our house, no electricity, no indoor plumbing. So our world as children was pretty insulated and pretty isolated," said Mankiller, who recalled her childhood in 2009 from the Cherokee Nation Headquarters in Tahlequah for the *Voices of Oklahoma* oral history website.

"We walked to school, to Rocky Mountain School, which was about maybe a two-mile walk and home every day. We farmed some things, most things for our own consumption, many things for our own consumption, and a few things to trade or sell to people. We have a natural spring on our property which served as the place where we got our drinking water. And we shared that spring with bobcats and mountain lions and wild pigs and other animals that would come through there, there were crawdads in it though it was a freezing-cold spring. So I lived there 'til I was eleven and then left to go to California and then came back in 1976."

Being asked to run for deputy chief with Swimmer came as a surprise. "Ross was a Republican. Ross was a banker. I came out of a social work, community-organizing kind of a background. I'm definitely a Democrat. And I think that what Ross and I shared is that we both believed in people. Anyway, when Ross asked me to run, I thought about it and, you know, didn't want to do it at first. And then it occurred to me that I had spent a lot of my adult life trying to convince people in positions of power to support things that I believed, and this would be an opportunity to allocate resources myself or do something myself.

"So I told him I would run. Ross had a rough time through that, because most of the people who were running on his slate and his council opposed my running with them on their team. I would have been on their team, not just his team. And there was a lot of opposition to it.

"I think part of it was because I was female and part of it was because of my work. I was running around rural communities talking about grass-roots democracy and things like that, and I was fairly outspoken. It was a chief, deputy chief, and a tribal council all ran together as a team, and they all said if he didn't get rid of me that they would not run with him. And he said, 'Fine, then Wilma and I will run on our own.'

"I asked Ross one day, 'Why do you want me to run with you?' And I remember he was behind his desk and he came over and he sat by me, in a chair by me, and he said, 'Because you love what you're doing and you're honest with money.' That's it."

In addition, as Mankiller put it, "Ross is the most secure male I know," but there were others who were not as secure as Swimmer in their masculinity.

"We would drive from Stilwell to Tahlequah and there would be a Swimmer-Mankiller sign, and someone would have painted out my name. So a lot of the sentiment was not toward him, but toward me. At another place going out on Highway 82, someone tried to burn down the sign.

"One night we came back from a meeting, I'd left my car in Stilwell, the tires were slashed on my car. Only two really scary things that happened to me: one, someone kept calling my house, and then there was a funny sound and then they'd hang up. And Charlie [her husband] listened one time and it was the sound of a gun.

"And then another thing which sounds innocent—you'd have to be there to understand how weird it was. But I was in a parade, and something caused me to look to the right and there was a guy standing against a wall doing a gun thing, shooting me with his finger. But it was the way he looked that was chilling. I think the most difficult time for me as a woman was that first time when I was out running for deputy chief and people just thought—I remember people saying I didn't have a snowball's chance, and just stupid things like that—were very hurtful. The conventional wisdom was that there was no way I could win. So then I won three times, three four-year elections."

There were those who were dubious about her leadership ability when Swimmer left for Washington, DC, but Mankiller proved to be effective by talking softly and acting decisively.

"I'm not a very divisive person. I don't believe in solving problems in a divisive way, so I just stayed steady, was respectful to everybody no matter how they treated me. I tried to keep them involved and tried to be diplomatic, and we eventually managed to get along.

"On the other hand, if I said I was going to do something, I did it and they saw that. I remember telling the Council in a very nice way that if they voted against our putting Job Corps in

Tahlequah that they were all opposed to—there's a fellow from Delaware County who wanted us to put up a community center and some kind of small business there, and I said, 'If you vote against this, I'll veto your project.' And he did, and I did.

"It was polite and respectful, but they also understood that I meant what I said. I remember telling people here who were running unlicensed, wildcat smoke shops, if you don't come in and start paying taxes and come under our purview and let us inspect your facilities and all that, then we're going to close you down. And they didn't, and I did. I think that they eventually began to see that I meant what I said."

Good advice for leaders, female or male.

For more of Wilma Mankiller's oral history—further lessons in leadership, and her specific advice to women—go to www.VoicesofOklahoma.com.

"How fast do you type?" I didn't type. They wanted me to type.

—NANCY FELDMAN

Nancy Feldman came to Tulsa in 1946 with high expectations. Married to a Tulsan and fellow law school graduate from the University of Chicago, Ray Feldman, she anticipated a positive reception from local law firms. For, as she recalled in 2012 from her home in Tulsa for the *Voices of Oklahoma* oral history website, "Oh, yes, I was very lucky because I had a rank in the law school that guaranteed me an excellent job." In Chicago, but not in Tulsa.

She ran smack-dab into a stone wall because she couldn't type. Type?

"'How fast do you type?' I didn't type. They wanted me to type."

The female attorneys reached out to help. "There was Drew Russell Mann, who had been a secretary and went to night law school, Dorothy Young. And Miriam Lashley came later. They all volunteered to teach me how to type."

Feldman's response was that she was a lawyer and that learning how to type was not part of being a lawyer. She tried a number of different firms. "There were a lot. And I had very odd experiences because I was young. I had lawyers say, 'Well, we could meet for dinner, and we could talk about cases.' I came home, and told Raymond and he said, 'What is this?' It was discouraging to say the least. Raymond was making $225 a month. We lived in a little apartment on Ninth and Main, which I loved. I was trying to get straightened out with what was a Jewish community. I had never... It was a time of a lot of adjustments."

One adjustment was to go, so to speak, to "plan B."

"In August, I marched out to the University of Tulsa. I stopped at a drugstore and called Sandra Kovach, who was head of the sociology department. I kept wondering, should I try to teach sociology or psychology? I decided sociology. Kovach hired me on a temporary basis, but I had to first go to J.E. Rogers, who was head of personnel for the board of TU. Rogers said, 'There are two jobs you could have. One would be an assistant to a judge, but I think you'd be happier teaching.'"

J.E. Rogers was perceptive—and right.

That "temporary" position lasted nearly four decades. "I loved it. I love teaching. I came home one night, and said to Raymond, 'Why are you practicing law? We could both make less money, and both of us teach, and it's such fun. I love it.' I had three months' vacation with the children, and I was home in the afternoon."

The irony, as Feldman pointed out, that despite undergraduate experience and attending Vassar and Northwestern University prior to her undergraduate and law degrees from Chicago, "I'd never had a course in sociology. I went straight to the library."

She had, however, *attended* many sociology courses at Chicago. "My life is so full of strange things. The leading urban sociologist in the country was a man at the University of Chicago. His daughter was named Nancy. She was a friend of mine. Her father had a Thursday-night graduate seminar on urban sociology. I would go in and just absorb. It was wonderful. The night before the last class, he said, 'I'm going to read your paper.' I said, 'You can't.' He said, 'Yes, I am, and you should be there and hear the response.' I was there, and it wasn't a bad paper. I love research. Then he called up a friend of his. He kept doing this. He'd say, 'I'm going to put a little girl in your class, just to sit in.' I sat in on all… Harvard and Chicago were the two best schools of sociology, so I just had that all there."

Fortunately for Tulsa, when she was stonewalled at Tulsa law firms, she didn't pout, and she didn't adapt to what were then the rules of the "game"; rather, she launched her life in a new and successful direction.

Fortunately for Tulsa?

Nancy Feldman's many credits include introducing the 1921 Tulsa Race Riot into her teaching curriculum despite being told to ignore the subject by TU administrators, challenging dairy companies who delivered milk to Tulsa public schools to date their milk containers, and leading the effort to expand arts education in Tulsa public schools. She founded what is now known as The Center for Individuals with Physical Challenges and the International Council of Tulsa, which would later become the Tulsa Global Alliance.

Along the way she learned an important lesson about femininity and men.

As one of only five women ("three of whom would not speak to me") in the University of Chicago Law School, she was often asked, "Why are you in law school?"

"I soon learned that if I said I would like to be a lawyer, that was a very unacceptable answer, so I'd say, 'There are more boys there than anywhere else and they had the longest vacations of any school,' and that was totally acceptable. And also that I wanted to sway the jury with my hips. By this time, I had realized, here were these three women so masculine wearing their neckties, etc., and I thought, 'I do not want to be like that,' so I started playing a role of this very feminine, stupid woman. It was a very strange thing, because they posted our grades and I was doing really well. I had boyfriends lined up. I mean, I'd always been okay but not a real popular kid. All of a sudden, it was because I was a fake."

Nancy Feldman had a stark realization that day: "I can manipulate these men by being fake. I lost respect for them totally, totally."

For more of Nancy Feldman's oral history—growing up in a Chicago suburb, teaching at the University of Tulsa, integrating Tulsa's exclusive Holland Hall school, and traveling the world—go to www.VoicesofOklahoma.com.

One of the things that distresses me is how politicians are not appreciated.

—NORMA EAGLETON

When Norma Eagleton graduated as valedictorian from Claremore High School in 1952, expectations were limited for young women. But Norma Eagleton would soon set those expectations upside down with a career in politics and public service. In 2016, she recalled those early days for the *Voices of Oklahoma* oral history website:

"We were blessed by some outstanding teachers, mostly women. In those days, women professionals aspired to be teachers. There were no women doctors or lawyers in Claremore when I was growing up. You hoped to be educated, you hoped to be able to teach if you needed to. Or all the girls took shorthand and typing in high school.

"We really expected to live exactly as our mothers had—to be married and have a family. But we took typing and shorthand in the event that our husbands died and we had to support ourselves. Or horrors, left us. So we needed some training, just in case. Young women anticipated that we would learn the skills and the values of our mothers and our life would be pretty much like our mothers' lives."

Fortunately, Eagleton had the opportunity to further her education, first for two years to achieve an associate's degree from the all-girls Stephens College in Columbia, Missouri, and afterward, with a degree in English and a minor in philosophy in 1956 from the University of Oklahoma.

"When John [whom she married in 1956] and I first moved to Tulsa, I did what most of my friends did and what I suspect my mother would have done. I was cookie mother and PTA mother and chauffeur to sports events and dancing class and those sorts of things. Tulsa, however, was a very well-organized town. They had a lot of auxiliaries, a lot of opportunities for volunteers to work. I was invited to join some of the young women's auxiliaries, the Tulsa Boys Home, the Cerebral Palsy Association, and such as those."

As the world began changing ("we had the women's movement; we had the environmental movement, and the world changed"), so did Eagleton's focus. "I joined the League of Women Voters. I was elected to the board and advised that I needed to have a portfolio. And it was suggested that I take the local government portfolio. So I said, 'Sure, I don't know much about local government, but I can learn.' What she learned was that Tulsa was being governed by a turn-of-the-century old form of commission government—and so she decided to help lead a campaign to modernize Tulsa's form of government. The campaign lost.

"After the election loss, Mayor Robert LaFortune appointed me to the city's utility board. That board had never had a woman, and he appointed me as the first woman to that board. I had learned in the League of Women Voters how to be a good public servant. You had important questions to ask: 1) Is it legal? 2) Who benefits? 3) Who pays? And this served me well. I began to ask questions, I began to read reports, I began to visit neighborhoods, and to understand what the city did."

This was to be Eagleton's city government apprenticeship that eventually led to running for office.

"Bill Morris, who was the finance commissioner, was very, very concerned about the flooding that development was causing in the city, and he decided not to run, and he said, 'Norma, would you like to run for my spot?' And I thought, 'Yes, I will.'

"My friends and I had worked on elections for years, and we knew how to run a campaign. And it was a fabulous campaign. I think I won every precinct in this city. Besides that, the city was kind of ready for a woman. I think they might have been a little embarrassed that they hadn't had a woman in public office before. But I didn't run as a 'first woman.' Remember, I was in lots of organizations throughout the city. The Boys Home, Cerebral Palsy Organization, the Red Cross, the United Way, the Urban League, I knew a lot of people. I knocked on doors, made telephone calls, made stump speeches all over Tulsa. Went on the television, had signs and slogans."

After Eagleton won: "on the day I arrived in City Hall on the executive floor, which was the eleventh floor of City Hall, there were two bathrooms; one was marked Executive, and the other was marked Women. There was a little bit of consternation."

There was no gender backlash, however, as "city government was very polite in those days. Politics was not nearly as scrappy as it is today. And city politics was very cordial, civil, and kind." And to an extent, nonpartisan. Eagleton, a Democrat, got her start in city government by being appointed by a Republican mayor to the utility board. A lesson she remembered when she reflected on the 2016 election results and its aftermath.

"One of the things that distresses me is how politicians are not appreciated. I hear people saying, 'Well, I'm not a politician, vote for me. I'm a businessperson.' Or 'I'm an individual citizen, I'm not a politician.' Politics is a noble undertaking. This is the government of, for, and by the people, and the people who select people to represent them in the difficult and challenging and interesting and important issues facing their life and facing our very survival. I think it's very courageous to present yourself to the public and say, 'I'm running for office. I'm willing to go to Oklahoma City or to City Hall or to Washington to try and represent you.'

"I regret the polarization today. This is terribly dangerous and counterproductive, and it's just wrong. The genius of America is compromise. In a big diverse country such as ours, a continental nation, we have to learn to talk together and compromise, because we're not going to see eye to eye. As I say, that's the genius of America. And one time when we couldn't compromise, we went to a bloody, bloody war, where 650,000 people died. The Civil War. The most bloody war in our history because of the inability to solve problems together because of the fragmentation, fracturing, polarization.

"So I believe government service is a high calling and it should be respected and protected and admired. I believe the goal of business is profit. The goal of government is keeping our society glued together."

For more of Norma Eagleton's oral history—earning a law degree, serving on the state's corporation commission, Tulsa's flooding, and the Black Fox nuclear plant controversy—go to www.VoicesofOklahoma.com.

And we found out, the big lie works because if you tell lies about something enough, you can actually prevail.

—PENNY WILLIAMS

One of the first things Penny Williams did after she arrived in Tulsa in 1968 after six years in Iran, the Sarah Lawrence–educated, from-a-solid-Republican-family woman, who was married to the president of a major Tulsa corporation, was to call up the president of the local chapter of the National Association for the Advancement of Colored People—the NAACP.

Sharing her fascinating life with the *Voices of Oklahoma* oral history website in 2012, Penny Williams recalled her first day in Tulsa: "That was day one. The minute I got back, I really had been living overseas for six years and not able to be involved in anything exciting going on in America. A lot that was really interesting, gripping was going on here, so I read the newspaper the day I came, and saw that Amos T. Hall had been elected the NAACP president, so I called him up. He was in the phone book. I called up his law office, and said I'd read where he'd just been made the president and I'd love to come, be involved in Tulsa, and get some advice from him on how I could help.

"That's how I met Don Ross and Shirley Scoggins, and Billy Roundtree and Bobby Eaton, and Bernard McIntyre, and Judy, all of those people I started working with on voter registration. It was a great call. He was the best. I really liked him so much, and he did eventually introduce me to all those people.

"I went to work for the League of Women Voters, eventually. But before that I had worked for Nelson Rockefeller for President, and found out how unpopular he was in Oklahoma. I thought,

'Oh, he's a good moderate Republican.' But he was thought of as far left here in Tulsa. The party was becoming more to the right at that time, little did I know. But it was, even though Henry Bellmon was very moderate, the party was growing in the other direction."

This was to have serious implications down the road.

Immersing herself in both politics and public service, Williams impressed state leaders with her connections and savvy. As a result, "Henry Bellmon originally asked me to serve on that Equal Rights Amendment committee. He and David Boren were honorary cochairs. I didn't even know what the Equal Rights Amendment was at that time, and I'm not embarrassed to admit it. But it was some twenty-seven words long and just gives a woman equal standing with a man when she walks into a court of law. That sounded pretty simple to me, and I was for it."

It needed to pass the Oklahoma legislature, and Williams learned bitter political lessons through that process.

"When I said I'd be on the state committee, I thought it would be a snap. David Boren and Henry Bellmon cochairing the committee? Come on. So, it wasn't any snap at all. There was a lot of resistance to it. And we found out, the big lie works because if you tell lies about something enough, you can actually prevail.

"People were told that women would be drafted immediately. That was the worst one. To give women equal standing in the court of law was not to draft women. And we would be forced to use the same restroom. Remember we had four restrooms in the train station in South Carolina? We'd have one, and it would be for men and women equally. There were a number of lies. The fact was a woman would never need this until she walked into a court of law and then she should have equal legal rights and she can't help that she's born a woman, right? It just seemed absurd that we would even have a law against her having equal rights in a court of law. At any rate, not only did we find out that the lie worked. We found out that that was just the beginning, and the day we lost the Equal Rights Amendment—I remember the lead opponent when I was being interviewed on television shifting her stance every time I turned my head, so I would have to look right into her eyes and she never went away. We went away. We folded our card file. We closed our office. We all went back to our lives and our children and our crabgrass in the lawn and whatever it is we were doing."

Penny Williams was, however, an exception. "Working for the Equal Rights Amendment, I had become close to my own representative, who was Republican. That was Paul Brunton, Representative Paul Brunton. He had told me when he was not going to run for reelection, he said, 'Hey, you ought to run for my seat.' Which I took as a joke. Then little by little, I began thinking about, you know, 'I really should do this.' I remember State Senator Finis Smith saying, 'It's better to work on an issue from here, where the door locks from the inside, then coming at us from Tulsa. Why don't you just try and get yourself elected?' So I didn't alone, but thanks to a lot of friends, we did win the seat."

That was 1998, and between 1968 and her return to Tulsa, she had not only worked on voter registration and the ERA campaign, she had also helped elect Norma Eagleton as the first voting member of Tulsa's City Commission, and James R. Jones to the US Congress.

She was to become known as a major legislative advocate for education, with one of her priorities being to bring higher education (beyond junior college) to Tulsa—the largest city in the country without a four-year public institution.

The opposition was formidable—legislative leaders represented the three major college towns that were recipients of the bulk of Tulsa's high school graduates: Norman, Stillwater, and Tahlequah.

Legislators led by Williams proposed a model that had been successful in at least two other states—a consortium made up of Oklahoma, Oklahoma State, Northeastern State, and Langston Universities. A consortium that evolved into OSU-Tulsa (at the undergraduate level), OU-Tulsa (graduate level courses), Northeastern State–Broken Arrow, and Langston in Tulsa.

A remarkable legacy for a remarkable woman.

For more of Penny Williams's oral history—living in Iran under the Shah, her involvement in successful political campaigns, and her dedicated support for education funding and legislation in Oklahoma—go to www.VoicesofOklahoma.com.

Good Sports

Although football is the current king for sports fans in Oklahoma—seemingly from peewee through college—baseball and basketball should not be ignored. For history shows there was a day and age when a town in Oklahoma would close its banks and its stores so its citizens could watch the local nine play ball, and once upon a time there was a Negro baseball league that put thousands in the stands. The stories of Oklahoma sports abound with grit and determination—from the sandlot, to the basketball court, and even to the owner's box.

A kid in a small town playing Tin Can, a businessman saving the national pastime in Tulsa, a studious basketball star, and a man who played when the only thing white on the field was the baseball itself—examples of Oklahoma's Good Sports.

But the epitome of my life was sitting in that locker room in the Astrodome for the '68 All-Star Game.

—JOHNNY BENCH

He has been called the greatest catcher in baseball history. And rightly so, for no one can compare with the Baseball Hall-of-Famer who was a fourteen-time All-Star, twice voted the National League's Most Valuable Player, and a key cog of the Big Red Machine—the Cincinnati Reds—winners of six division titles, two National League pennants, and two World Series crowns.

Johnny Bench of Binger, Oklahoma.

This baseball great first learned how to "play ball" through a game called Tin Can, and even as far back as the second grade, he knew what he wanted to be when he grew up. He looks back upon a day in 1968 as the epitome of his career—and that day has nothing to do with titles, pennants, or championships.

He told *Voices of Oklahoma* about the early experiences that ultimately led him into the sport of baseball.

"We played a game called Tin Can. It was an old Milnot can, they had the church key to poke up the top of it. Just make the holes and then you've got a bat that was splashed in half at the end so you had a flat surface.

"And you'd throw the can and if you hit it past a certain area and it's a base hit and a double. And if you hit it farther, it was a triple and a grand slam if you hit it into the shed. After you hit it a few times you could throw a curve ball, screw ball, sliders, and by the end of the game it was just one solid, round mass of tin or metal. You know, we basically played with our bare hands, which made it fun and gave us a chance to really start learning to hit breaking balls and change of speed. And it sort of molded me to become what I was as a hitter."

Molded him to the point that as early as the second grade he had set his future course.

"When I said, 'I want to be a major league baseball player,' they laughed.

"Nobody really ever even thought about that. In the eighth grade, Mrs. Tate asked everybody what they wanted to be, and I again said, 'Major league baseball player.' And they laughed again.

"But I grew nine inches in the next two years so when I was a junior Mr. Rhodes asked the class, and when I said 'baseball' they didn't laugh so much this time because I was starting to really do well at baseball."

"Do well" was an understatement. Signed by the Cincinnati Reds in 1965, he was on the road to becoming Rookie of the Year when that "most memorable day" happened in 1968.

"The epitome of my life was sitting in that locker room in the Astrodome for the '68 All-Star Game. And I'm sitting at my locker, I was picked as the third catcher by Red Schoendienst, who's the manager. And I'm sitting there staying out of the way 'cause I'm just twenty years old, I mean, I'm just trying to stay out of everybody's way and not spike anybody. I mean, these guys are going by me, these are the future Hall of Famers and everything else. His National League All-Star teammates included Henry Aaron, Felipe Alou, Steve Carlton, Don Drysdale, Curt Flood, Bob Gibson, Don Kessinger, Jerry Koosman, Juan Marichal, Willie McCovey, Pete Rose, Ron Santo, Tom Seaver, Rusty Staub, and Billy Williams.

"I'm sitting there at my locker and across from me in the locker room was Willie Mays. Willie looked at me and he got up and walked over and he pointed at me and said, 'You should have been the starting catcher.' And that was it, I didn't need anybody else. That was the most important time in my life, the most important thing anybody could have said."

Bench's admiration of the players who made the game what it was in those days didn't end in 1968. "And then the next year in '69, I asked Roy Sievers, who had played with Ted Williams, if he would take me over and see if Ted would sign a baseball for me. I went over with him. Ted said, 'Sure,' and he signed the ball. I thanked him, I walked out of the locker room and looked at the ball and it said, 'To Johnny Bench, a sure Hall of Famer, Ted Williams.' Ted Williams knows who I am.

"I remember when Sandy Koufax was doing the baseball games, and he walked in and said, 'Hello, Johnny, I'm Sandy Koufax.' And I said, 'God.' I mean, Sandy Koufax knows who I am. Ted Williams knows who I am. Willie Mays said, 'You should have been the starting catcher.'

"It's pretty awesome, isn't it?"

Yes, it was, and it is, and it is still oh so human for a kid from Binger, Oklahoma, who grew up to be a star-struck star.

For more of Johnny Bench's oral history—his growing-up years playing with older players, his father's advice, and playing with the Big Red Machine, go to www.VoicesofOklahoma.com.

No, I don't want to be in the baseball business, but Tulsa needs a baseball team.

—BILL ROLLINGS

On one level, the two of them made television's *The Odd Couple* look like identical twins.

The prime mover was a successful construction executive, and his partner was a world-famous entertainer, a Las Vegas show star and an occasional guest host on Johnny Carson's *The Tonight Show*.

But on a different level, they were the perfect pair for partnering up in owning a baseball club, specifically the baseball club that saved professional baseball in Tulsa.

Bill Rollings, the construction company owner, had played professional ball for the Beaumont, Texas, Exporters, a Double-A team in the Texas League, after his discharge from the navy following the Korean conflict.

And his partner, with a 49 percent ownership in a fledgling baseball team, Roy Clark, was the kind of baseball fan who told the *Voices of Oklahoma* website that if he saw kids playing baseball by the side of the road, he might stop his car to sit and watch.

It certainly helped that they knew one another and that Rollings had at one time played in Clark's Children's Hospital Celebrity Golf Tournament. Their combined efforts saved baseball in Tulsa.

The tradition for America's greatest pastime in Tulsa dates back to 1905 for professional baseball, and to the early 1890s for amateur teams representing the city. There was even a time in the city's earliest days when the banks, the shops—well, just about everything in town—would close so people could turn out for the game of the day.

But in 1977, all of that was about to come to an end. The owner of the fabled Tulsa Oilers, a Triple-A farm team of the St. Louis Cardinals, had decided that baseball, for Tulsa at least, was history. The team—lock, stock, balls, and bats—moved to New Orleans, because the owner could not reach an agreement with the county on repairs to the aging ballpark on Tulsa's fairgrounds.

A representative of the fairgrounds contacted Rollings, who had done construction work for the city and for the county, and as Rollings shared with the *Voices of Oklahoma* website in 2012, asked if Rollings could help land a baseball team for the city.

Rollings called a friend, Brad Corbett, one of the owners of the major league Texas Rangers, who asked, "'Bill, are you wanting to be in the baseball business?' and I said, 'No, I don't want to be in the baseball business, but Tulsa needs a baseball team.' He said, 'If you want to be in the baseball business and Tulsa needs a baseball business, you'll have to do it, and I'll get you a baseball business.' And that's how we got started in the baseball business."

While there were numerous details to be worked out, including asking Roy Clark to join in as a part-owner, it culminated with a Tulsa team, named the Drillers because the Tulsa Oiler name belonged to the fellow now in New Orleans. The new Drillers team debuted with an exhibition game between the Houston Astros and the Texas Rangers at the ballpark on the fairgrounds. A ballpark that looked good and shiny, but the paint and polish turned out to be lipstick on a pig. The new era of professional baseball in Tulsa actually started with a crash.

Tulsa baseball historian Wayne McCombs was there on April 3, 1977, to work the electronic scoreboard. "It was Sunday," McCombs recalled for the *Voices of Oklahoma* website, "I think the game started at one. I think I skipped Sunday school and came to the ballpark. It had rained all morning, but about 11:00 the weather started to clear, and the game was going to go on. There were about five thousand people in the stands, and that's about all it could hold. The game began, and then it started to cloud up again and began to lightly rain.

"Then in the second inning, it began to rain again and there was some thunder. Then I heard what I thought was a heavy thunderclap. What had happened, part of the stands had given way. The people had come up underneath the stands where there was a roof on the right-field side, between home and first base. They got in an area that was too weak for 2,500 people to stand on. About seventeen, eighteen people fell about twenty feet onto a concrete walkway.

"The game was stopped for quite a long time. Ambulances came. The accident occurred near the clubhouse of the Houston Astros. About ten or twelve of those men came out and carried people in their arms out to the ambulance."

Seventeen people ended up in hospitals, the stands ended up being demolished, and yet, with temporary seating, the Tulsa Drillers, in its first season, would end up winning the first half of the Texas League Eastern Division in 1977.

Baseball was not only back, but due to Bill Rollings, it had never really left.

For more of Bill Rollings's oral history—the first precarious seasons with attendance averaging 700 to 800 per game in a makeshift ballpark, how a new ballpark was finally built, and how baseball flourished again in Tulsa, go to www.VoicesofOklahoma.com.

We were the only college team to ever beat the Harlem Globetrotters.

—MARQUES HAYNES

From a three-bedroom house in Sand Springs featuring insulation by panels made from cardboard boxes and wallpaper from the local newspapers, to the Basketball Hall of Fame. Such was the improbable leap made by a man who set the basketball world on fire with his dazzling dribble technique.

Marques Haynes was the player who made that jump, with a lot of help from a mother who preached education first and basketball second.

He recounted his journey to the *Voices of Oklahoma* website in 2011 from his home in Plano, Texas.

"We just had that one school in Sand Springs called Booker T Washington, named after a great black educator. I went there from kindergarten all the way through high school.

"One day I was reading the *Pittsburgh Courier*, which was a black newspaper, and I saw where a fellow by the name of Pop Gates was being paid $250 to play basketball. I couldn't imagine that someone was being paid to play basketball. That's when I started concentrating a heck of a lot more on basketball," said Haynes.

Concentrate he did, and he rose from his role as a ninth grade mascot, "what you would call a student manager now," to his first big break in his sophomore year.

"The team was going to the National Negro High School Basketball Tournament, which was being held in Tuskegee, Alabama. I was the ninth man, and the ninth man didn't get a chance to make trips outside of the state. But one of the other players got sick and couldn't go. They stopped by my house that morning at 5 a.m. to ask me if I could go. I told them yes, and my mom got me ready and I went down to Tuskegee with them. We ended up winning the National Negro High School Basketball Tournament.

"I ended up making second-team All-American, and I got the chance to meet Dr. George Washington Carver. That's where his laboratory was, and I met Eleanor Roosevelt."

Higher education was the next step, with academics rising to the forefront of Haynes's focus, rather than basketball.

"Our church gave a twenty-five-dollar scholarship to the student member of the church that had the best grades. I couldn't help but win, because I was the only one from my church that was graduating that year. So, I got the twenty-five-dollar scholarship. I went up to get it and they told me they would send the twenty-five-dollars to the school of my choice. Langston was the school of my choice.

"I got to Langston and I went to get my twenty-five-dollars. They told me to sign a piece of paper and I signed it. I went to put my hand out for the twenty-five-dollars and they said, 'No, that's for your tuition.' I thought—what am I going to do now? I remembered one thing, my oldest brother who went to Langston used to work on the yard for a fellow named Uncle Bill. So, I went to Uncle Bill and asked him if he needed another worker. He heard my name and realized he had hired my brother and he told me to come on. He asked me, 'What can you do?' I said, 'I can cut grass.' He said, 'Can you fix a lawn mower?' I said, 'I can take them apart and put them back together.' He said, 'Well, your brother couldn't do that.' I said, 'He probably did a lot of things I couldn't do.' He said, 'Let me see you do that.' I took that sucker apart and put it back together so quick that he told me I was hired even before I finished it."

Lawn mowing and other part-time jobs helped Haynes's journey through Langston, which was almost interrupted by an encounter with a famous basketball team…until he remembered his mother's continued focus on his grades.

"The Harlem Globetrotters were going to play in Oklahoma City, but the team they were going to play canceled out on them. They got a hold of our coach, Zip Gayles, and asked if our team would substitute and play against them because the other team wasn't going to make it. Zip said, 'Yeah, we'll play against you.'

"We got into OKC at the old auditorium. We warmed up before the ball game, and all of the coaches and the captains would meet at center court. Their coach told our coach, 'We'll beat you when we play you, but we won't make you look too bad.' Zip told us, 'Hell, make us look bad?' He said to us, 'You guys shoot your best shots—you guys know what to do.'

"We thought, 'Okay, let's get it on.' We got it on and what happened at the end of it, we were the only college team to ever beat them. Langston University beat them by four points." And the Globetrotters were not doing their usual comedy routines. "They were for real. They were playing straight up. They wanted me to travel with them after that. I said, 'No, man, my mom would kill me if I left school now. I'm graduating in May.'"

The Globetrotters kept in touch, and Haynes started out with the Kansas City Stars.

"It was like a farm team for the Globetrotters. I did my dribbling act and shooting act and all of it, making, I think, about $250 a month.

"A Hawaiian team was supposed to play the Globetrotters in Oakland, California. The Kansas City Stars were playing in the same deal. The Stars were supposed to play the first game, and then the Globetrotters were going to play the second game. I was on the Stars at that time. The Hawaiian team was supposed to play the Globetrotters in the main event. Somehow, they were beating the Globetrotters. Winfield Welch, the traveling secretary for the Globetrotters, one of owner Abe Saperstein's trusted employees) asked me, 'Do you want to play against the team from Hawaii?' I said, 'Sure.' So, I went on and got dressed and I took one of the Globetrotters' places. As soon as I got in the game, I started firing away. I looked up and we were 10 points ahead of them.

"That's when I joined the Globetrotters."

From that game in Oakland to playing more than twelve thousand games and entertaining millions in 106 countries with his trick shots and masterful dribbling, to a basketball legend: Marques Haynes.

For more of Marques Haynes's oral history—going to movies in Tulsa, his years with the Globetrotters, and forming his own Harlem Magicians, go to www.VoicesofOklahoma.com.

As it was, they had the Negro League, and when they come here, if they come a day ahead of time, they would end up at my house.

—PORTER REED

There was a time in the history of baseball when, for a certain league, the only thing white was the baseball itself. It was the Negro Baseball League—the league of legends—Cool Papa Bell, Josh Gibson, Satchel Paige, and Jackie Robinson. Unfortunately, "major league" baseball and its farm teams were closed to Bell and Gibson, but fortunately, Paige and Robinson made the "show," as it is known.

And a longtime Oklahoman encountered nearly all of the Negro League legends—playing against and with some of them. In its day, Muskogee, Oklahoma, was a major stop on the Negro League baseball barnstorming circuit. As a child, Porter Reed saw the Kansas City Monarchs, the Chicago American Giants, the Memphis Red Sox, and other Negro League teams play in Muskogee during the 1930s. As a teenager, Reed himself played on the local team battling the Negro Leaguers when they came to town. And when the Kansas City Monarchs came through, he would play both with the Monarchs and against them.

During his long baseball career, Porter played with the Birmingham Black Barons, the Muskogee Cardinals, the Detroit Wolves, the Houston Eagles, the Minneapolis White Elephants, and the Los Angeles Stars. He played with such famous names as Jackie Robinson, and he batted against such names as Satchel Paige.

On June 29, 2016, Reed shared his memories with the *Voices of Oklahoma* website at the Three Rivers Museum in Muskogee, OK. He was ninety-three years old at the time.

Most vividly he recalls that he was very familiar with the Kansas City Monarchs long before he even played baseball— when in Muskogee they practiced on a field some fifty or sixty yards from his very own front door.

"The Kansas City Monarchs, and all the teams that come here, they would practice right in front of my house.

"My third-door neighbor was named New Joseph. He played third base for the Kansas City Monarchs. When they practiced there, they would come across the street to my house and get water and use the bathroom and everything. It just made it handy. I was the handy boy, you know, like a bat boy. I was gettin' water and gettin' twenty-five, fifty cents, a quarter.

"I wanted to be a third baseman real bad when I was a little ole boy. And I would stand behind New Joseph, which was that All-Star third baseman for the Kansas City Monarchs. He'd field 'em, ground balls. A lot of 'em he'd just move out of the way and I was caught, you know, tryin' to play third base.

"As it was, they had the Negro League, and when they come here, if they come a day ahead of time, they would end up at my house."

In later years he would meet Jackie Robinson, who broke the "color line" in baseball when he was signed by the Brooklyn Dodgers.

"The one mistake that the Kansas City Monarchs made on Jackie Robinson—you know what that was? He didn't have the arm for shortstop. That's why they put him on second base. And the reason why he did so good in shortstop with the Kansas City Monarchs, he had Buck O'Neil at first base. He scooped him and saved him. Those good first basemen, they can save an infielder. But Jackie Robinson is like Satchel, he had it all down pat."

John: Did you see him in person?

Porter: They eat in my house and ate at my table and used my bathroom.

John: What was he like to be around? Was he a fun guy or—

Porter: No, he didn't like prejudices, he was well educated and knowin' he wasn't bein' treated right. But that man Branch Rickey of the Dodgers talked to him and showed him where he—he could listen. Now, you could say, "Now, if you do this tomorrow…" let him know he wasn't goin' to stay in the same rut, he would understand. There's a place up there for him. Jackie, he was like Satchel, he was just a natural, he was just a good, natural baseball player.

Reed notes that Rickey broke the color line with Robinson to not only put a Hall of Fame–caliber player on the field, but also to put fans in the stands. Reed explained the math: "Now, the reason why Branch Rickey got him, the American and National Leagues had an All-Star Game. They played in St. Louis and had 34,000 people at the All-Star Game. Negroes played in Chicago, their All-Star Game, the East and the West, 56,000.

"Now, right here in Muskogee, they had the Reds, Cincinnati owned the Reds and they was playing C ball. They had a ball game right over here at this civic center. Be three and four hundred, maybe five hundred people. If they had six hundred people they had a sellout. Kansas City Monarchs come here and the game's at night and we had three and four thousand."

Reed didn't like prejudice any more than Robinson, but he had learned to live with its reality. "I remember a time in Muskogee, blacks couldn't go across Main Street to the east side unless they worked over there. And when a policeman arrests you in Muskogee you didn't give no sass, you'd get your—whupped. I mean, get it whupped.

"You listen to this now, you're not goin' to change things. As long as there is a world there's goin' to be prejudice… You try to live your life, try to get along with your fellow man, try to raise your family, you try to do right. You see, I ain't been around here a long time for nothin'. I know when to hold 'em and I know when to fold 'em."

For more of Porter Reed's oral history—his early days playing baseball, batting against Satchel Paige, his career as a bootlegger, and why he eventually left that pursuit, go to www.VoicesofOklahoma.com.

At the Pinnacles of Power

While Oklahomans have been close to the presidency— in the case of Speaker of the House Carl Albert, next in line when Vice President Spiro Agnew resigned—it is more likely that the state's statemen, two in particular, were close in the sense of advisors and confidants.

Two men who served in that role were Henry Bellmon and Fred R. Harris—one a Republican and the other a Democrat. A third Oklahoman who served with distinction in the nation's capital had to overcome a personality that kept him quiet in school—David Boren was shy. Had it not been for a teacher and a kindhearted woman on whose door he knocked while making his first run for public office, David Boren's life could have remained just that…quiet.

And then President Nixon started to cry.

—HENRY BELLMON

Oklahoma statesman Henry Bellmon was there the night President Nixon announced that he was resigning from the highest elective office in the country. He shared memories of that night with *Voices of Oklahoma* from his ranch home near Billings in April 2009.

The former governor and US senator from Oklahoma met the future president in 1958. His first impression was not particularly favorable.

"He came to Oklahoma City when we had the Republican National Committee meeting there." Nixon was vice president at the time, and Bellmon said, "My first impression of Dick Nixon was that he was not a very strong individual either intellectually or orally or any way you measure politicians. He seemed to be, I don't want to badmouth the man because I came to like him a lot but he seemed like he was a little shallow, kind of giddy. He didn't impress me as a strong leader."

After Nixon lost his bid for the presidency in 1960, he also lost an election for governor of California and then famously declared that the press would not have him to kick around any more. Several years after that Bellmon met him again. "In 1966 Nixon had established himself as kind of an outstanding international lawyer. He was in a big law firm and he had gained his self-confidence and he had become really kind of a different person. When I met him, I was impressed by what I took to be the changes in him."

Bellmon was impressed enough to become one of the future president's earliest supporters, which provided him with access to what some thought would be Nixon's inner circle—an inner circle that met only twice—six years apart.

"The first meeting was about three weeks after he was inaugurated. Rose Mary Woods, who was his secretary, called and invited me down for dinner at the White House. When I got there, I found out there were about twenty-five of us there, all Nixon supporters before the New Hampshire primary. Nixon came in and shook hands with us all and talked to us and slapped us on the back, and we had a very pleasant and jovial evening. He told us that this was the Early Birds Club and that he was going to be in touch with us because we helped him get the nomination when nobody else would. Everything was fine. Well, the next meeting of the Early Birds Club was before he resigned.

"The afternoon before he resigned, Rose Mary Woods called up—he hadn't announced he was going to resign yet. She invited me down to dinner at the White House again. I went down, and it was the same group. We hadn't met for six years. This time we met in the cabinet room where there was this long table with chairs and there's one high-back chair where the president sits. We didn't know that he was going to resign, but we had a premonition that he would. There was no conviviality. It was awkward.

"Nixon came in with his head down and he never spoke to anybody or patted anybody on the back or asked anybody, 'How's your wife?' There were no exchanges of any kind. He went right around the table and sat down at this tall black chair, and when he did that we all scrambled around to get a seat at this big table. Nixon looked up and he welcomed us and then he started to talk. He talked about what he had tried to do and where he thought he had succeeded and where things hadn't gone right. He thought he had done some things that he may be remembered favorably for. Words just poured out of him for probably forty-five minutes, then he stopped talking and he looked down.

"Then he raised his head up and looked around and said, 'I hope I haven't let you down.' And then he started to cry. And when he did he jumped up from his chair and more or less hurried up to the end of the table and then down the hall. He had scheduled an appearance on all three major channels, I think, for eight o'clock that evening. And we were worried that he wouldn't be able to get his composure, but he did. He made the announcement that he would be resigning at eleven o'clock the next day."

For more of Henry Bellmon's oral history—his World War II near-death experience, his decision to enter public service, and his fight on behalf of education funding in Oklahoma, go to www.VoicesofOklahoma.com.

Johnson thought that John Kennedy was a lightweight and said that to people.
—FRED HARRIS

Fred Harris occupied a unique place in US politics in the mid to late 1960s. Not only was he a liberal senator from the conservative state of Oklahoma, but, as he recalled for the *Voices of Oklahoma* website, "*Time* magazine wrote that I was the only person in Washington who could breakfast with Lyndon Johnson and lunch with Hubert Humphrey and dinner with Robert Kennedy, which was true and they all knew it."

Harris was first elected to the US Senate to fill the unexpired term of Senator Robert S. Kerr in 1964—narrowly upsetting the legendary former University of Oklahoma football coach Charles "Bud" Wilkinson.

Lyndon B. Johnson, who won his own race that year—by a landslide over Republican presidential nominee Barry Goldwater—played a role in Harris's election.

Harris shared that story in 2012 from his home in Corrales, New Mexico, where he was enjoying life as a professor emeritus of political science at the University of New Mexico.

"Johnson came to Oklahoma toward the end of the campaign to dedicate a dam. It was one of Bob Kerr's Arkansas River navigation projects. I couldn't be on the platform because this was a presidential visit and I was a candidate. Johnson didn't want to be associated with candidates in tight races because he didn't want to put his prestige on the line and it was obviously a close race."

Later, as a fund-raiser in Oklahoma City, Harris would find himself face-to-face with the president due to the ingenuity of his press secretary. "Under the fairgrounds stadium there is a big space where we had a big private party/fund-raiser. I was invited to that and Johnson was there, but it was closed to the press. There were drinks and it was a standing-up crowd milling around.

"Ross Cummings, my press guy, I don't know how in the hell he did it, because this was a Secret Service thing and you had to get through the Secret Service to get in there—but Ross got in there with a cameraman and a soundman.

"So, we were in there and Johnson is walking around with his scotch in hand. He's shaking hands and he comes over to me and he says, 'How are you, Fred? It's good to see you!' I'd gone to

Washington and had my picture taken with him so he knew who I was. About that time, Ross Cummings put a microphone right up in the president's face. The camera started, and you could hear its whirring. He said, 'Mr. President, would you say a word about Fred Harris?'

"Well, you could tell that Johnson was just madder than hell. He was thinking to himself, *I said no press*, but he was conscious that the sound was on and the camera was whirring. He handed his drink to somebody, and he turns to me and shook hands with me. Then he looked back at the camera and these are his exact words, because we used them in an ad. He said, 'I need Fred Harris in Washington. Send me old Fred and we'll charge hell with the bucket of water. Old Fred will bring home the bacon and tack the coonskin on the barn door.'

Elected to Washington, Harris began moving in the circles of the Johnsons, the Hubert Humphreys, and the Robert (and Ethel) Kennedys. He had a front-row seat to the spectacle of bad blood between the Kennedy clan and Lyndon Baines Johnson.

"Robert Kennedy thought Johnson was corrupt. He also never forgave Johnson for raising John Kennedy's health as an issue at the 1960 Convention, which he did, and it was true. He did have Addison's disease, and probably the treatment itself is what caused his thyroid to atrophy as we now know. Johnson knew all of that.

"Johnson thought that John Kennedy was a lightweight and said that to people. He thought that Kennedy had not amounted to anything in the Senate and was a womanizer, although Johnson was too. But all those kinds of things Kennedy knew, and he hated Johnson for it. He also thought Johnson was bought and paid for by people like the Halliburtons. He thought he used his office to make money with a television station and other things.

"Meanwhile, Johnson thought Robert Kennedy was a rash sort of snot-nosed kid who was vicious and who had said and done a lot of things against him too. Then this thing happened at the convention—I heard it from both Johnson and Kennedy. Old Man Joseph Kennedy figured out, quite rightly, that Kennedy could get elected with Johnson on the ticket, and probably couldn't without Johnson. So, John Kennedy did what his father said and offered the vice president nomination to Johnson and Johnson accepted. Incidentally, Johnson told me that Robert Kerr came busting into his room and said, 'They tell me you are thinking about running with our boy from Boston. If you do, I'm going to take my .30-30 and shoot you right between the eyes if you are thinking about that.' Walter Reuther, the head of the United Auto Workers union, and others were just crazed by this idea. But Johnson stayed as Kennedy's running mate.

"From Robert's standpoint, he thought Johnson wasn't worth a damn as vice president and that his advice was no good."

John: Did they cut him out a little bit? He had to be a lonely man.
Fred: Oh yes, oh, terribly. Robert and Ethel, they just loved to talk about Johnson.
John: Did they make fun of him?
Fred: Yes, it was just terrible. It was so weird to me. But Kennedy, he knew that I was a supporter of Johnson's and liked him.

And President Johnson clearly knew what was going on.

"One time I was at Hyannis Port having dinner with Robert Kennedy. The phone rang in the other room and Ethel went to answer it. She came back to the dining room and said to me, 'You're in trouble now, kid! President Johnson's on the phone for you.' I thought it was a joke, but it wasn't. I got on the phone, and he said, 'How are you doing, Fred?' I said, 'Just fine.' He really didn't say much of anything. Obviously, the only reason he'd called was that he just wanted me to know that he knew where I was."

Politics can, at times, be like a soap opera.

For more of Fred Harris's oral history—about championing human rights around the world, running twice for the highest office in the land (from an RV), and how close he came to being his party's vice presidential nominee, go to www.VoicesofOklahoma.com.

...I mean, I was just really in tears over it.
—DAVID BOREN

State legislator, the winner of a gubernatorial upset, a United States senator, and the thirteenth president of the University of Oklahoma, David L. Boren has had an illustrious career. And along the way he has been the recipient of enough medals and plaques to fill the wall of a good-sized office.

But among the plaudits he most prizes is one that came with no medal or plaque. It was the recognition he received for his role in freeing Nelson Mandela, and his support of democracy in South Africa, that touches Boren the most. Captured on video tape, this moment in time was to help him, years later, calm a potentially volatile situation on the OU campus.

This is the story as Boren shared it with *Voices of Oklahoma* in 2016.

"Senator Sam Nunn and I went to South Africa together. That's where we first became really acquainted with Ambassador Edward Perkins, our ambassador to South Africa, the first African American ambassador to be appointed to South Africa. We became great friends. He briefed us a great deal. He had been working for the release of Nelson Mandela. Although originally committed to nonviolent protest, Mandela was eventually sentenced to life in prison in South Africa for conspiring to overthrow the state. The ambassador thought we could be helpful when we were meeting with the president of South Africa and other officials there. We really pushed the agenda of Mandela's release. And we continued to work on that after we got back to Washington.

"I went to see then Vice President Bush, well, I think he was then almost president-elect. And he announced a change in policy. Reagan had allowed trade with South Africa, but Bush was going to announce a change that we would boycott South Africa economically until they released Mandela and moved toward democracy. And I was very much involved in those discussions.

"By the way, being in South Africa, and seeing how the people were so exploited and not given equal opportunities for—they weren't being educated. Walter Sisulu was in prison with Mandela and I met with his wife. She was kept under house arrest. She was guilty of fighting for equal education for black children. That was one of the first things I asked President Bush to ask for when he became president, for her ability to travel and be released from house arrest.

"I was sitting in her little house where she was under house arrest in Soweto, and I told her, 'Someday you're going to be sitting in our living room and you're going to come into Washington and you're going to come and see us.' 'Oh, I'll never get there,' she said. And I said, 'You will.' A year and a half later she was sitting in our living room.

"President Bush Sr. had authorized me to speak to the South African government to demand a release and to say that his policies would be based upon the things they did. So, I got very heavily, heavily involved in the whole campaign to free Mandela. And then Ambassador Perkins would secretly send me messages of what I needed to tell the president, or what I needed to tell the secretary of state about his negotiations and where the pressure points were. We all worked together. The president then, not knowing that I was working with his own ambassador to do what he said to bring the pressure; Mandela was released. And then, of course, he came to the United States.

"Ted Koppel, the journalist, had a town hall meeting on the air for three hours from Harlem. It was quite an extraordinary event. Mandela was, of course, the centerpiece of it all. I was invited to go up and be there, kind of at the back of the stage, there must have been forty people on this big stage and an audience of ten thousand in this big auditorium.

"All of a sudden Ted Koppel said, 'Senator Boren from Oklahoma is here, and I want him to stand up.' I stood up, and Koppel said, 'I want everyone to know that he worked very hard to get sanctions put back on South Africa until they agreed to free elections and free Mandela. And that he's played a key role in this.'

"And he said, 'Senator, how is it that you got involved in that? Is that popular in Oklahoma politically for you to be for putting sanctions on South Africa?' I just said, 'Well, Oklahomans are a moral people and we know what's moral and what's not. What was going on in South Africa was immoral, and I absolutely feel that the people of Oklahoma would share my feelings about this.'

And then, I guess, it's one of the most remarkable things that ever happened to me in my lifetime, Mandela stood up.

"He started applauding, and then he turned to Ted Koppel and said, 'Ted, I've giving Senator Boren a standing ovation for the role he's played, not only in my release, but in bringing democracy to South Africa.' You know, it was just the most touching, gripping moment, I mean, I was just really in tears over it. I don't think I've ever in my whole career been paid a greater compliment than that."

Fortunately, Boren was given a video tape of that sequence of events.

"You fast-forward to other things that happened in your life, like a racial incident that happened on our campus where we were put under the spotlight nationally and with some of our students, especially our student athletes, we had a gathering after that. And the Athletic Department called over and said, 'Do you have a tape of what Mandela said to you?'"

When the tape was played for the athletes, it gave Boren the credibility he needed to both defuse and resolve the situation.

For more of David Boren's oral history—the broom brigade that swept him into the governor's office, his service on the Senate Select Committee on Intelligence, and his years as president of OU, go to www.VoicesofOklahoma.com.

In 1987, we sat down, and we started our family foundation.
—LYNN SCHUSTERMAN

Charles Schusterman started Samson Investment Company in Tulsa, and there were lean years for him and his wife, Lynn, who recalls, "I can't call it hand-to-mouth, but everything went back into building the company."

And build the company they did. Its success gave them the opportunity to implement the Schustermans' spirit of giving—something that had started years before with borrowed money.

"In 1987, we sat down, and we started our family foundation, the Charles and Lynn Schusterman Family Foundation. I remember sitting in the basement of our home and making the decision to start the foundation. Our kids then were still in high school and we were talking to them and trying to involve them a little bit in starting the foundation because we thought that it was very, very important to give back to others.

"I vividly remember sitting in Temple Israel in Tulsa in 1967 and listening about the needs in Israel, about the '67 War. We went to the bank and borrowed $500 to give to Israel.

"The two of us have always cared about giving back and being involved.

"The focus of the foundation, and it still is to a large extent today, is the philosophy of helping someone to be able to cross boundaries from which they were born. So other people could really learn and improve their lives and other people's lives because of the foundation."

An idea first implemented with a $500 bank loan.

Righting Wrongs

A legacy of segregation was written into Oklahoma's constitution. It was the bitter law of the land. And despite hardcore holdouts to the wheel of justice that declared that separate but equal was anything but, Oklahoma overcame its segregationist heritage without firehoses or people screaming vicious racist insults at schoolchildren. That's not to say it was easy, but Oklahoma had leaders who wanted to right wrongs the right way.

I was more afraid of Clara Luper than I was the sit-in movement. She was a strict disciplinarian.

—JOYCE HENDERSON

At a time when civil rights giants gathered to plan marches and protests across Oklahoma City, Joyce Henderson was a high school student who served as the song leader on Saturday mornings at that city's Calvary Baptist Church.

One of Henderson's high school teachers, Clara Luper, was one such civil rights giant, as she led the nation's first lunch counter sit-in demonstration, with Henderson as a participant.

Years later, in March 2016, in a replica of the living room of Clara Shepherd Luper created at the Oklahoma History Center, Joyce Henderson shared with the *Voices of Oklahoma* website what happened on that late August afternoon in 1958, when thirteen youngsters along with Clara Luper went to Katz Drug Store in Oklahoma City. At that time in history, blacks could order food "to go," but they could not sit down in the diner.

"Or, you could go in many restaurants, get your food, and eat in the back. And when I say 'the back,' I mean, outdoors, you could not eat in the facility. And that's the sad part. You could buy anything you needed in their store, but when it came time to eat, you could not eat in the store. Not only that, you couldn't go to the bathroom unless you were going to a separate bathroom. You think back and say, 'How much money did you spend to keep us separated?' Not only did you have restrooms for blacks, you had to divide those restrooms, male, female, so you just went through a lot of trouble to separate us."

John: So, on that day they sat at the counter and the waitress says?

Joyce: "We cannot serve you."

John: And Clara says, "We'd like thirteen Cokes, please"?

Joyce: "We want thirteen Cokes." They refused. In fact, I would imagine they got so nervous they didn't know what to do, because it hadn't happened where you just wouldn't get up after being asked to leave because we're not going to serve you. I'm sure everybody panicked. And again, we didn't have social media so that we could share what was going on at that time. But the word got out, and that was the beginning.

Clara Luper stood firm, as did the thirteen children with her at Katz. Henderson notes, "We had strict rules and regulations on how to behave, how to conduct ourselves under these circumstances. Because of that, we never had the kind of violence like you had in some of the other states when they were trying to integrate facilities. We didn't have dogs sicced on us. We didn't have water hoses on us. We did have those who decided, 'Well, we'll just spit on you.' They didn't do it to me. You did have those who decided, 'Well, I'm going to pour water on you.' We did have those who would call you bad names. But we had been instructed how to react and we were not to be violent."

John: The police were obviously called to this original sit-in.

Joyce: Well, they were there to make sure we didn't cross the line. The one thing that we learned later, Miss Luper had a relationship with the Oklahoma City Police and with the police chief. And they would know what we were going to do. And because of the relationship, he would instruct his policemen on how we were to be treated. Because of that relationship, nothing got out of hand. And I believe that was the key to our nonviolent sit-in movement here in Oklahoma City. Now, when you think about the thirteen, when you are a child you are an obedient child. Because if Clara Luper told you to do something, you were to obey that. And I tell people today, "I was more afraid of Clara Luper than I was the sit-in movement." She was a strict disciplinarian. And if my history is correct, they opened their doors to blacks in three days.

John: They did relent, yes. As a matter of fact, they had thirty-eight outlets in Missouri, Kansas, and Iowa. They relented in all of those stores.

Joyce: That's right. Someone made the decision with Katz Drug Store, "The right thing to do is to integrate our restaurants." And they did that, which opened the doors for some others, but many others became pretty stubborn too.

Indeed, that was only the beginning of a movement that would sweep across the segregated South—starting with the nation's first sit-in in Oklahoma City.

"The seed was planted because of children saying, 'Let's do this.' We found out that we were the first nonviolent sit-in on the books in the United States. And they have that now as a record, because at first we thought it was Greensboro, North Carolina. And history showed that it started in Oklahoma City."

For more of Joyce Henderson's oral history—her experience with the Jim Crow laws, her years as an educator, and her participation in the March on Washington, go to www.VoicesofOklahoma.com.

We had national publicity because this had never happened—voluntary integration was a whole new thing in the United States.

—NANCY MCDONALD

In 1954, the United States Supreme Court unanimously ruled that "separate but equal" education laws were inherently unequal. That signaled the end to *de jure* (by law) segregation. The next year, the Court ruled that desegregation should proceed "with all deliberate speed."

The Tulsa Public Schools Board of Education apparently did not receive the memo. For as school volunteer Nancy McDonald remembers for the *Voices of Oklahoma* website, "About February of 1971, Federal Judge Dougherty said to the Board of Education, 'You desegregate Booker T. Washington by 1973.'"

Booker T. Washington High School was the traditional African American secondary school in Tulsa—a school that the Board of Education historically had seemingly wanted little to do with. As a matter of fact, it (and Carver Junior High School) were built and owned by Tulsa County.

The Board carried on its attitude of neglect for nearly two full decades following the Supreme Court ruling, until sanctioned by the federal court.

Seeing the turmoil created around the country by "forced bussing" to achieve desegregation/integration, school patrons such as McDonald looked for alternatives. But there were no school patrons as willing as McDonald to step into leadership roles to end segregation.

Working closely with administrator Bruce Howell, McDonald and her corps of volunteers helped to show the way at Burroughs

Elementary School and Carver Junior High. It wasn't always easy, but it was accomplished.

High school integration was a much more challenging step.

"The Board of Education had the plans for the desegregation of Booker T. Washington, which were very interesting. One plan was they would use Booker T., Central, and Edison high schools. If you were in the tenth grade, you would go to Booker T. and if you were in the eleventh grade you would go to Edison, and in the twelfth grade you would go to Central. Well, that was great for everybody that lived outside of that district, so that didn't work.

"Then they had a plan where they would draw little pockets around the city, but you would never know where those little pockets would be. If you lived in that pocket, you were sent to Booker T. Washington for one semester, so that was continuously changing. That created too much anxiety in the community. Another plan was they would have a lottery. And that was too risky, and people didn't like that. So Bruce Howell said, 'Do you think we can do this voluntarily?'

"He asked me if I would chair the recruitment. He told me H.J. Green was the principal. He had talked to H.J. and Granville Smith (Green was white, Smith was black) about changing positions at Hale and Booker T. And H.J. had agreed, and he wanted me to meet him. So, working with Bruce Howell and H.J., an advanced and unique to Booker T. curriculum was designed. H.J. went around to all of the nine high schools and talked to kids about what they would like to have happen in their high schools. And we had everything from every language to basket weaving to sophisticated advanced courses. Had we been able to open Booker T. the next day, we would have had our enrollment. But the parents had to sign off on that. And so, when those applications were taken home, we had nine returned and we had six hundred white kids that we needed."

The goal was 1,200 students evenly split between black and white. A respected leader from Tulsa's African American community, Julius Pegues, was in charge of black recruitment; McDonald had the other 50 percent—a recruitment effort that actually united politically divided partisans.

"You had to convince people, first of all, that it was safe. That was their one question: Are my children going to be safe? We had all of the liberal families, and then we had the conservative families who felt that it was their duty, so it was an interesting mix. They thought it was their duty to be part of this. I think that this was sort of a calling. They wanted to live out their respect for fellow human beings. We had a lot of that conservative, fundamental, I need to be a part of this, this is my calling, this is what Jesus is expecting me to do, I am going to be a part of that. So, we had an interesting mix of kids, which sometimes can be a little challenging. So how did we recruit? It was tough. But I finally came upon the model that the community meetings were not working. This had to be done in very small groups of people. If I had one parent, if you volunteered to go to Booker T., I would ask you to host a coffee and invite your friends. And so, that summer, H.J. Green and I attended seventy neighborhood meetings to recruit.

"It came about the middle of August and I was still short about 167 white kids. Joe Williams, chairman and CEO of the Williams Companies, who funded most of this, came up with the idea that we would develop a brochure. I remember distinctly, we would send it to 22,542 kids that attended Tulsa public high schools. It was a great brochure. Our logo was '167 men and women needed.' We had volunteers put that newsletter together.

We mailed it under the All Souls Unitarian Church stamp because that would save us money.

"So it was a morning in August, and Pat Bradley and I were going to take down the mailing to the bulk rate mailing station. I unloaded them all and took them in there. This man in charge looked at them and said, 'This doesn't look like a church mailing to me. I am not going to approve this.' I thought, 'Wow, what do we do now?' I asked to see his supervisor and a supervisor walked through the door, an African American. He looked at it and he said, 'It looks like a church mailing to me.' And he let it go, and that's how we got the mailing done that day.

"We sent out these brochures and we were successful. We had people apply. It was right before school started. We had 600 whites and 600 blacks, and we went before the Board of Education and said, 'We have completed this. It's ready to go.'

"We had national publicity because this had never happened—voluntary integration was a whole new thing in the United States. I remember standing with H.J. the morning of the school opening and wondering if the kids would actually get on the bus and come, but they did."

Today Tulsa's Booker T. Washington High School ranks among the Top 100 in the United States.

For more of Nancy McDonald's oral history—her service on the Magic Empire Girl Scout Council the year that three young scouts were murdered at camp, her founding of the Tulsa chapter of PFLAG— Parents, Families, and Friends of Lesbians and Gays, as well as her other experiences in volunteerism, go to www.VoicesofOklahoma.com.

As I remember it, everything was segregated when I came here in 1953.

—DAVID BERNSTEIN

If there were a "Mr. Executive Director Award" in the city of Tulsa, David Bernstein would have retired the title. Over his award-winning career, he served as executive director of three of Tulsa's influential and prestigious organizations: the Tulsa Mental Health Association from 1969 to 1973, the Community Service Council from 1973 to 1985, and the Jewish Federation of Tulsa from 1985 to 2000.

Managing nonprofit organizations and public service were not his ambitions following graduation from Fairleigh Dickinson University in Rutherford, New Jersey. "My degree was in English literature; Shakespeare and English literature is worth two cents on the market when you get out of college," recalled Bernstein for the *Voices of Oklahoma* oral history website in front of a live audience at Temple Israel in June 2011.

His plan had always been to continue on to law school. "I took the law exam and I was accepted at Rutgers and NYU. I was set to go to NYU, but it was a tough time because my mother died in 1952, the day after the presidential election. She had cancer for quite a while so it was a tough time in our family when she was ill. My sister was a nurse and took care of her. I just didn't have an appetite to go to school, I guess—I don't know."

He opted to join the workforce instead and accepted a job with Rayco, a seat cover company. "My job was to train the people in Tulsa whom Rayco in New Jersey decided were ignorant. They thought a young kid out of college could train them. I came here to open the store and to hire people to work in the shop. We made seat covers and we made convertible tops." As manager of the Rayco store at 3815 East 11th Street, Bernstein found himself in a world far different from his native New York and New Jersey.

"As I remember it, everything was segregated when I came here in 1953. Movies were segregated and so were buses. I hired a foreman who was black. I didn't know anything about segregation. Coming from New Jersey, I assure you I didn't know anything about it. I had to select a new crew and then from them I had to select a new foreman. I was there maybe two or three weeks and I picked a foreman who happened to be black. He was the best worker I had. He ended up being a minister in Tulsa.

"I took him to a drive-in restaurant and he said, 'You are not going to get served.' We waited and waited, and he said it again, 'You are not going to get served. They won't serve me.' We never got served and finally I found out why—it was because I had a black friend in the car and they weren't going to serve me. This was on a Sunday night, because we worked seven days a week. By Monday morning, none of those white guys showed up to work. They all quit because they weren't going to work for a black supervisor.

"The store had a waiting room, a sales room, and a shop. We would take the car into the shop and put the seat covers on and drive it out. I noticed that when a white kid would drive out and park the car, the customers would walk out and see the seat covers and see that everything was fine and then they would come in and pay. If a black guy drove that car out of the shop, they would come down to see the seat covers and then open up the glove compartment and make sure everything was there. That was just a bias that was built in in this part of the country. It was very, very hard to deal with as a young idealistic Easterner."

John: The segregation that we are talking about and the prejudice, was it mostly toward blacks? Did you feel or see any of this toward Jews in Tulsa?

David: Yes. Everyone knows about Southern Hills Country Club, so it's not a secret. The whole area of Southern Hills, the neighborhood was to keep Jews out. Jews and dogs were not really wanted in that area. Southern Hills Country Club didn't allow Jews to be members, simple as that. So, before I came here the Jewish people built their own country club. That's where Meadowbrook Country Club came from. They earned money. They became businessmen. They wanted to live the life they saw their compatriots living, so they had to build their own place. That was terrible to see.

John: Did you ever try to hide your Jewishness? Or consider changing your name?

David: No. I personally didn't. If someone needed to do it to get a job, I understand their doing it, but I didn't have to do it, and I was proud of who I was. I grew up in a religious atmosphere culturally with all Jews and I was proud of being a Jew. The oil companies here were not hiring Jews. Texaco and those large companies would not even interview Jews.

John: Were they turned away?

David: Yes, they were turned away. I didn't apply for one of those jobs, but when I applied for the job as director of the Community Service Council, which was a United Way agency, the United Way did a search to make sure my being Jewish, I wouldn't interfere with anything that they were trying to do, which was raise money from these high-level executives. They were wondering if I would put them off.

So, they called a meeting and I met with half a dozen of the top executives in Tulsa. I purposely wore my hair long and everything else, but I still got the job.

That experience was the continuation of Bernstein's career, which included fighting prejudice in any form.

For more of David Bernstein's oral history—including helping to develop services for Tulsa's growing Hispanic and Cuban population, the creation of the YWCA's Multicultural Service Center, and developing the city's twenty-four-hour suicide prevention hotline, go to www.VoicesofOklahoma.com.

I don't know how many college presidents there are who have had a burning cross put in their front yard, but I awakened to one.
—BEN HENNEKE

Although his name isn't found on any buildings on the University of Tulsa (TU) campus, his impact is undeniably evident.

Ben Henneke's impact on TU began as an undergraduate in 1931. Before he graduated, he wrote the Hurricane Fight Song and founded the campus radio station, KWGS. Following his hiring as its president in 1958, the university earned full accreditation, buildings were built, and the north campus opened.

Equally important in the eyes of many (but not all), TU was integrated.

Henneke shared his experience of being caught between the proverbial rock and a hard place with the *Voices of Oklahoma* oral history website in September 2009.

"We were as white as you could be until the government said it was wrong to be different. We were obeying the Oklahoma law that set us up. Although Indians were permissible, there was a state charter that said that blacks were not. So we were law-abiding citizens. Then the federal government said to everybody that they may be law-abiding, but you are obeying the laws that have recently been passed. The United States said that we must admit black people as well as white people. So we had a problem, because the state of Oklahoma did not agree with the federal government, but the University of Tulsa did.

"Being a pioneer is a very interesting experience. Our experience, I think, is worth telling. After the war, we had set up a school for black people in the black community. The Booker T. Washington High School ran courses at night for black students so that they could make up work that they would have had, had they been in Tulsa.

"That branch offered a multitude of courses. One year it offered a course in sociology. It didn't have enough students enrolled to make it pay off, therefore it could not continue. You had to have at least six people in the class to break even. The university treasurer saw to it that nobody was teaching a class with five people in it, because we would lose money and we couldn't do that.

"So here was this class losing money, and the teacher, quite innocently, said to his other class, 'This is really very strange. I am offering this same class on the north side and I am going to have to quit it because there are not enough blacks in it to make the class requirement. If they could come to this class, I could just teach one class.'

"One of the people in the class whose name I never got, which breaks my heart, some young man in the class, because it was an enormous class, said, 'Why can't they join us?' And the faculty member said, 'It could cause a riot, because it's against the law in the state of Oklahoma. I am perfectly willing for them to join us, but somebody here might object to it. If I was to take a vote, I am sure somebody here would not be very happy. I will be glad to take a vote and see what happens. I think I can have the blacks from the north side join us here. But I don't want any one of you to not want it to happen. You are obeying the law if you vote against it. We will take a vote. Raise your hand if you are for it. That's great. It looks as though everyone but one held up his hand, so we will continue on as we were.'

"Then he said to the young man, 'It's surprising that you were talking about what to do and you are the one person that did not hold up your hand.' The young man said, 'I didn't hold up my hand because what we should all do is not act like it was something strange. She is a person just like you and me.' Evidently there was a woman in the north campus class, so essentially he was saying 'she' is as good as you and me. I remember his speech so well that I have to explain how he was able to say 'she.' He said, 'She is just as good as we are, and she deserves an education just as we do. She probably is just as sweet as all the women in this class are, but she's getting a half-baked education over there because don't tell me that our professor does as good a job the second time around to three or four people as he does to us the first time around with fifty people.

"'I don't want to see her embarrassed or treated like that. Other schools are segregating them and putting them in different parts of the room, and I don't want to have her come to this class and be in a different part of the room. We are really quite on the horns of a dilemma. If we greet her, we are making her special. And yet, how is she going to know that we just sit where we want to? What can we do?'

"The teacher said, 'I will guarantee you she will come to this class if this class votes 100 percent.' They did, and she came and graduated.

"OU was the only other school that would admit a black student other than a black school. They roped off a section, and a magazine wrote a story about it. This kid did not want that kind of a story about the class he was attending. So we didn't rope anybody off. Every other night school teacher was told that they could teach at night school and have black students. So they passed the word along to the black community that they could attend classes at TU at night. All we had to do was to get them to break the barrier that we had. The barrier was the town.

"There are rednecks in the world—people who do not like what's going on. Every time we had a new thing, we had a new fight. I don't know how many college presidents there are who have had a burning cross put in their front yard, but I awakened to one.

"I wasn't trying to be any leader. We just agreed with the government. I mean, the guy who put the cross in my front yard evidently didn't agree with the government. But our trustees never took a vote. They just did things such as say, 'That drummer you got sure has helped the band!'"

For more of Ben Henneke's oral history—working with Ed Lacy on finding the right football player to integrate the team, the first words said on KWGS, and other tales from the halls of higher education—go to www.VoicesofOklahoma.com.

Mentors Matter

Les Lang. Bessie Lee Harris. Arthur D. Harrison. Three people who were hardly household names—except in their own households. One was a gym teacher who spotted a youngster's athletic potential, one a sixth-grade teacher and principal who believed that a child should know about life outside the classroom (what was called "civics" in its day), and another a high school teacher who forced a student to take chemistry and encouraged his writing.

Without the mentorship of their students, one could build a case that the world would not have had the pleasure of enjoying an Olympic champion, a perceptive newspaperman and editorial writer, and a musician, writer, and chronicler of Woody Guthrie.

But because Les Lang, Bessie Lee Harris, and Arthur D. Harrison cared as much as they did, Oklahoma now knows of Bart Conner, Alex Adwan, and Guy Logsdon. Thank you, Les, Bessie, and Arthur.

I think you might have some potential to do something in gymnastics.

—LES LANG, BART CONNER'S FOURTH-GRADE PHYSICAL EDUCATION TEACHER

B art Conner, an Olympic gold medalist in gymnastics, remembers that while he had physical talents not common to most youngsters, it took a perceptive teacher to suggest that he channel those talents into becoming a world-class athlete.

Conner spoke to *Voices of Oklahoma* from his office at the Bart Conner Gymnastic Academy in 2013 in Norman, where he graduated from the University of Oklahoma. He remembers headstands and walking on his hands at an early age.

"I was small and strong and pretty light. The key to gymnastics is your strength-to-weight ratio. I was small and strong—you know, I had the school record in pull-ups. Every gymnast did. We always used to joke at every high school or grade school or elementary school, when they put up the record in the President's Council on Physical Fitness and Sports, the kid at the top of the list was always a gymnast. Because we're light and we're really strong.

"So, I could walk all around the house on my hands. I could walk around a basketball court perimeter on my hands. It's just something I loved to do. When I was probably five, six years old, I'd see if I could hold a headstand for five minutes while I was watching TV. You know, just little physical challenges. It was an important sort of catalytic moment for me when I was ten years old, because in school PE class in the Chicago area, you had six weeks of wrestling, six weeks of baseball, six weeks of gymnastics, six weeks of swimming. All the schools offered a variety of sports.

"And my fourth-grade PE teacher, a gentleman named Les Lang, noticed that I was pretty skilled at the acrobatics and the tumbling. And he said, 'How would you like to go see what gymnastics is all about? What if I get your parents' permission? I'll take you and your brother over to the high school on a weekend and you can see what gymnastics is. Because I think you might have some potential to do something in gymnastics.'"

For the fourth-grader it was love at first sight.

"So that was forty-four years ago, and to this day, I can remember what it looked like, what it smelled like, and what it felt like to walk into that gym. I came around the corner behind the bleachers, I saw the rings and the parallel bars and the trampoline and the mats and the vaulting, and I just thought, 'This is where I belong.' Because to me, it looked like a high-tech playground with cool stuff to swing on and fly off of. It didn't look to me like a structured sport at the time, it just looked like the coolest place to play. I was captivated right then at the age of ten. And I just felt like this is where I belong.

"I'd played lots of sports growing up. Growing up in the Chicago suburbs, of course, we played football, basketball, baseball. I was in Pop Warner football. Played hockey because the Chicago Blackhawks were a big deal in Chicago at the time. But gymnastics was just the thing that, you know, made my heart soar, and I knew it from the beginning."

John: Because one man reached out to you and spotted
   your talent.
Bart: In a way, that moment, one man with goodwill, good
   intentions, it sort of set my life on a path that has defined
   everything about me and everything I stand for. I'm

grateful for that. We work with a lot of kids, and you don't know who's going to be that one person that might just say the right thing at the right time. So, I'm grateful. We still remain friends.

"I think your life is a series of small choices. Maybe there's a few big choices along the way, but those small choices, that day when he said, 'Hey, I want to see if I can help these kids, show them what gymnastics is about.' And then my parents saying, 'Yeah, go, go on over there on Saturday morning at the high school and see what it's about.' And then, you know, I walked in there. I look back now and I see what a monumental moment it was.

"But it was just a small choice to go over at ten o'clock on a Saturday morning and see what the high school kids could do on the rings. That has set the direction of my life all these years later."

Ultimately, that direction—the Olympics—was also suggested at an early age, and it shaped the entire course of Conner's life.

"My first term paper, when I was in eighth grade, was about the history of the modern Olympics, because my dad wanted me to understand that the whole foundation of the Olympics was to bring the world together in peace; try like crazy to win, but at the same time, foster acceptance, tolerance, relationships, friendships around the world, always with a sense of fair play and good sportsmanship at the core of it. So, I learned that at a very early age. And that really has defined my life in many ways.

"You know, I married a young lady from Romania, Olympic gold medalist Nadia Comaneci. I mean, these are things that only happen because of the Olympics. My parents growing up in a time, and me for part of my life, in the Cold War period, we saw many countries as enemies. And yet the Olympics somehow bridged those gaps and said, 'Come together and let's foster a sense of acceptance and understanding that you might not otherwise get.' Sports is a great place to learn that."

For more of Bart Conner's oral history—his unusual choice to go to the nineteenth-ranked gymnastic school, his Olympic gold win, the Conner Spin, and his business ventures, go to www.VoicesofOklahoma.com.

...when I got to OMA (the Oklahoma Military Academy), I kind of had in mind that I wanted to be a writer...

—ALEX ADWAN

Alex Adwan got his start in journalism at the Oklahoma Military Academy, but his initial inspiration to become aware of the world beyond his hometown was sparked while he was still in elementary school. The resultant combination was a distinguished journalism career that earned him a place in the Oklahoma Journalism Hall of Fame.

He described that initial impetus to become a writer to the *Voices of Oklahoma* oral history website in 2010.

"I had a lot of good teachers in my hometown of Maud, and I remember especially Miss Bessie Lee Harris. She was the principal there and taught sixth grade. I was kind of teacher's pet. She got me interested, believe it or not, in politics and the important things in civics, in other words. My grandmother was also a teacher, and she talked a lot about important things. So I was introduced to pretty serious business at a pretty tender age, I guess. I skipped the seventh grade and went into the eighth grade. And then from there I went to Oklahoma Military Academy. That was in 1944."

OMA pointed him in the writing direction.

"Well, it was a military academy. There was no hazing in the physical sense, but for practical purposes we were made to stand with our knees bent and our arms out in front of us for long periods of time, and it was rough the first semester. But I came to like the place. I go to these reunions now and we look back on those days, and I'd say, 'How can anybody feel any affection or have any good memory of a place that was so much like a prison?' But we did like it. I did pretty well there, and I was editor of the school newspaper, the *Guidon*. And one year was editor of the *Vedette*, the yearbook. Got a kind of start in journalism there."

The writing seed, however, had been planted even earlier than that.

"I can't remember all the details of this, but my grandmother wrote a little poem and she had it published in the local paper there at Maud. I would have been maybe nine years old or so, or maybe less than that, a little kid. Then she said, 'You need to be a writer.' So, I guess even when I got to OMA, I kind of had in mind that I wanted to be a writer or maybe a newspaper man or something."

While he loved OMA, he had a rebellious streak. "The last year I was there, I accumulated at one time the highest number of demerits that had ever been issued without being kicked out of school. I had a friend and he had a car and left and came to Tulsa, that was against the rules. And got back in two hours later, early in the morning, and there was a TAC officer waiting for us when we got there. So it was not an offense of moral turpitude, but taken quite seriously by the commandant. I lived through that and graduated from high school there in 1946, and from junior college in 1948. Then I went from OMA to University of Oklahoma School of Journalism."

Adwan's goal was the newspaper business, and following service as a tank platoon leader in the 45th Division in Korea, he began his ascent up the journalism ladder: the *Seminole Producer*, the *Wewoka Times*, and the *Pauls Valley Daily Democrat*. He became copublisher and managing editor of the *Seminole Producer*. From 1960 to 1967, Alex was with United Press International, serving as a bureau manager in Tulsa, Houston, and Oklahoma City. He covered Houston's new space center in the early 1960s, reporting on the last of the one-man orbital space missions and the beginnings of Project Apollo, the program to send astronauts to the moon. He joined the *Tulsa World* as a Washington correspondent in 1967, became an associate editor in 1972, and the editor of editorial pages in 1981. On his retirement as editorial page editor in 1994, Adwan had been named senior editor.

With his long and distinguished career, Adwan's words to aspiring journalists take on special meaning.

"First of all, be a good writer. Because to be a good communicator you have to have something to communicate, and that starts with getting something down on paper, writing, and those skills related to that. Beyond that, I don't know of any technical education that I can recommend, because I don't know where the technology is leading. But I would advise anyone who is going into it to learn all of the skills of the show business side of journalism: how to speak on a platform, how to perform on television, and how to address a group of people. Because it has now become show business, there is a show business aspect to it that is more important than some guy like me sitting down at a typewriter and batting out his story and putting it on the wire."

Adwan cited a prominent example at the time of his oral history contribution. "In order to be a good Washington correspondent, say you've got a job like David Broder, the distinguished political writer who wrote for the *Washington Post*, he's had to learn in his old age, almost, how to appear on television and handle all those things, and he does very well at it."

The end result? "There're a lot of writers, successful people today, who go out and they write a column or a story for a newspaper and then turn around and do a regular TV appearance. You see that all the time. That's what I would tell journalists of the future, that they need to learn those things."

For more of Alex Adwan's oral history—encounters and interviews with presidents, senators, Speakers of the House, and his support of public education— go to www.VoicesofOklahoma.com.

———————

And I can hear my daddy say, "Oh, he has no talent."

—GUY LOGSDON

Recognized as one of the country's leading authorities on Woody Guthrie and a holder of multiple academic degrees and numerous honors, Guy Logsdon would have had a far different life had the recommendation of his uncle been heeded. But fortunately, it was ignored, and when combined with the education and encouragement of a high school teacher, Logsdon went on to a distinguished career. He shared his early educational background and thoughts on Guthrie's legacy with the *Voices of Oklahoma* oral history website in 2010 from his Tulsa home.

"About two years before my mother died, and about seven years after I'd finished my doctorate at the University of Oklahoma, I was down visiting her. And just the two of us were there. And she said, 'You know, your uncle Claude,' who was the oldest of the Logsdon family there, 'wanted us to put you into a home for mentally retarded children.' I said, 'What?' She said, 'Yeah.' I said, 'Why?' She said, 'You wouldn't talk.' 'I wouldn't talk? I don't know how to shut up now!' 'No, you wouldn't talk.'

"And about five years ago in the *Tulsa World*, there was an article about late-talking children. They're now doing a tremendous amount of research and they know that late-talking children come from musical families, and often are musically talented. And in the past years, many have been placed into homes for mentally retarded children. And that explained many things to me. I was never encouraged musically like everyone else in the family.

"I wanted to take piano lessons, and up the road and up a hill the Lucas family had this big, old, old-time rock house, it's now been torn down, but she was a piano teacher. And my sisters took piano up there. So I went up by myself and said, 'I'm going to take piano.' Second grade. She had a sister who was a bit detached up in the head and she loved dogs, which means she had a good soul. She always picked up stray dogs and she'd lead them. You'd see her walking all over Ada with three or four dogs on leashes. I went up one time after about the fourth or fifth lesson and those dogs came out after me. And I remember rolling down that hill, screaming like mad, with those dogs jumping all over me. I never went back for piano lessons."

Once visitors heard music at the Logsdon home and asked if it was coming from Guy. "And I can hear my daddy say, 'Oh, he has no talent.' And I lived with that 'no talent.' I wanted to play the guitar. 'You're not smart enough to learn to play the guitar.' So my brother had a guitar, and every day in high school after school when others were doing homework, John was working at the furniture store making money. I'd go home, and I taught myself to play the guitar. So my guitar playing is strictly self-taught. As well as I had the privilege of knowing Eldon Shamblin, Tommy Allsup, and others. And I learned by watching."

He also learned from a dedicated high school teacher.

"Arthur D. Harrison was a teacher in Ada High School. When I was a sophomore, this was when you went in and the teacher said, 'Well, you're going to take this and you're going to take that.' And they signed. He said, 'You're going to take chemistry.' I said, 'No, I'm not.' 'Yes, you are.' I said, 'No, I'm not.' 'You're going to college, you're going to take chemistry. You have to.' I said, 'No. I don't think I'll be going to college.' 'I don't care, you're taking chemistry.' And he enrolled me in chemistry and sophomore English. And he was the head of the high school annual, the faculty member in charge. He taught chemistry and he taught high school English. He was the art teacher.

"When I was editor of the high school annual, as a senior, working under him, I found out he had five master's degrees and was qualified to teach any subject in Oklahoma. He directed choirs, he taught home economics to the girls, he did a little of everything. If they needed a spot, he took it for that year. Mr. Harrison had the greatest influence on me of any teacher I ever had. I think I made a D in chemistry. But in English, I still remember, this is when you bought your own textbooks, sophomore English, first day, he said, 'Take your books back and get your money back from the bookstore. You're going to have a year of grammar because all other English teachers are too lazy to teach you grammar. They're going to teach you literature. I'm going to teach you grammar.' We didn't look at Shakespeare, we didn't look at anyone. We had grammar. And I'm not perfect, but I guarantee you, I know a little about grammar as a result of Art Harrison. He taught art. I had two years of art with him. I was photographer for the annual in my sophomore year. Worked with him there. English, chemistry, anyway, he made me editor of the high school annual. Art Harrison was an amazing teacher.

"Many years later, I was working on Woody Guthrie's life, I go through the 1929 Panther Annual in Okemah, open it up, and there's Art Harrison, who taught Woody Guthrie. I went back many years later and interviewed him about Woody. And he taught typing and business. That's where Woody—Woody was a speed typist. The man who helped him was Art Harrison. So I feel honored that a man who taught Woody I also had as my greatest teacher. And a tremendous influence on me, because I was still a late-talking child in the minds of many. It explains many things that I even went through in high school. But I'm fortunate."

Logsdon's interest in Guthrie resulted in a book coauthored with Guthrie's sister, Mary Jo Guthrie Edgmon, *Woody's Road*, and a lasting impression on Logsdon.

"I happened to believe as Woody believed. I believe in the working people of this country. I happen to believe that the destruction of the middle class and the working class is killing this country. And if we had Woody with us today, he would be singing his heart out trying to save the working people of this country. You know, I've had people say, 'Labor unions are terrible.' Well, how the hell do they think the middle class came about? It didn't come through the generosity of the wealthy. It came through people joining together, demanding rights."

For more of Guy Logsdon's oral history—being investigated by the FBI, his interest in cowboy songs, and his association with Bob and Johnnie Lee Wills—go to www.VoicesofOklahoma.com.

On Being Remembered

How do you want to be remembered?

A question nearly everyone wants to be asked, and certainly looks forward to answering. Whether one's greatest achievement is in the raising of a family, or the governing of a state—people seem to have an inherent desire to be remembered. Not only by name and by face, but by deed.

Countless songs from "Try to Remember," to "I Remember You," celebrate this human trait. Include *VoicesofOklahoma.com* among the celebrants. And on the following pages, join in the celebration of those whose thoughts on being remembered range from the seemingly flippant (yet upon second reading very profound) to thoughtful and deep. Each one reflects the personality of its speaker and the very human condition of remembrance.

WILLIAM POGUE

One common trait among those with "the right stuff," was an ability to literally fly in the face of risk. This "test pilot mentality" was a prime factor in favor of America's early astronauts. For in the early days of the National Space and Aeronautics Administration there were not only unknowns, but the mysterious unknown unknowns. Into this atmosphere entered William Pogue from Sand Springs, Oklahoma. And before he retired from NASA he made two space walks (one for a record seven hours) and conducted numerous scientific experiments. The author of several books, including an autobiography entitled, *But for the Grace of God*, Pogue had a succinct response to the question, "As you look back on your life, how would you like to be remembered?"

Just a dumb old Okie that doesn't really care about taking a chance.

HENRY ZARROW

The first son of immigrant parents from Latvia (Russia), Henry Zarrow had nothing in life handed to him. As his entrepreneurial spirit and intelligence enriched him, he dedicated himself to handing out to others. Through the Anne and Henry Zarrow Foundation, the lives of many—in particular children (education being a primary concern), the homeless, and the poor—have been enriched. He told *VoicesofOklahoma.com* that his wife, Anne, was the biggest influence on his philanthropy and if asked to sum up his life:

I would say that I am the luckiest man I know of that God let me live this long. And I appreciate every day. I'm happy He let me live.

JOYCE HENDERSON

One of thirteen children under the supervision of her high school teacher Clara Luper to participate in one of the country's first lunch counter sit-in demonstrations, Joyce Henderson would follow in her mentor's footsteps. Not only as an educator, including twenty years as a high school principal in Oklahoma City, but as a leader with the NAACP. She responded to the question, "How would you like those sit-in demonstrations to be remembered by today's young African Americans?"

I would like for them to know that there were those of us who had the courage to make a change. And because of what we did, and because of the opportunities they now have, don't take it lightly. Take advantage of it. Don't say, "I don't want an education." Don't say, "I don't want to be a productive citizen."

ROBERT J. LAFORTUNE

Tulsa's thirty-first mayor, Robert J. LaFortune, first served as commissioner of streets and public property from 1964 to 1970 on Tulsa's City Commission. During his terms as mayor, he played key roles in the development of the Tulsa Port of Catoosa, and forging the public/private partnership that resulted in Tulsa's Performing Arts Center. His memories shared with *VoicesofOklahoma.com* concluded with, "So, then overall as you are remembered, you could be remembered as what?"

Good ol' Bob. I've never wanted to get a lot of recognition—I don't think that's necessary. People know what I have done. I see it every day, I don't go almost anywhere in Oklahoma that I don't see somebody that remembers my face or my name or some association with the LaFortune family. That's a proud moment for me. Especially when I'm with some of my grandchildren and someone says, "Hey, Bob, isn't that you? I remember you. We met 20 years ago." Or somebody will come up and say, "Hey, Bob—remember I worked in your campaign?" I say, "My campaign? That was 30 years ago!" Those are proud moments obviously and not because you did anything about it—it's just that they have a favorable impression of what you did.

JOHN H. WILLIAMS

The man Bob LaFortune forged the public/private partnership with that brought Tulsa its Performing Arts Center was businessman John H. Williams. His remarkable career included a cover story in *Business Week* magazine during his days of building the Williams Companies. His legacy will long be remembered.

I am proud of what I've been able to do here in Tulsa. I don't brag on it, but I'm glad the name Williams is going to be around for a while. It's an old, corny thing—it's a different thing when your name's on the door. It's quite a different responsibility. You want to be very careful that that name is preserved. I am proud that Williams is, I think, a better-known name in Tulsa today than it was before I came here 60 years ago.

DAVID BOREN

College professor, state legislator, governor, US senator, and pres ident of the University of Oklahoma. But, really, David Boren, how would you want to be remembered?

For what I've done, not to help myself, but what I've done to help other people—that's what you want to be remembered for. Another thing in our society that concerns me, we might be losing civility in other things in our society. Someone asked me what I wanted to have put on the base of a statue that they have at OU for me that I won't let them put up until after I'm departed. I said, "I want you to put on the base of the statue, 'Never underestimate the power of kindness.'" Because I've seen it in my life, kindness comes back to you many times over. And, you know, the way we treat each other, in many ways, will determine the future of our society and the real strength of our society. As much as even military power, economic power is, but how we treat each other is going to really determine the real strength, the bedrock strength of this country. So, I hope that will be on my tombstone.

WILLIAM K. WARREN JR.

The cliché "like father, like son" can prove to be true. It is spot-on in describing the lives of William K. Warren Senior and Junior. For when Senior's dream of giving back to his adopted community of Tulsa became a reality with the opening of Saint Francis Hospital, William K. Warren Jr. not only shared that dream, but expanded upon it. His stewardship as long-time chair of The William K. Warren Foundation has seen the growth of a 275-bed hospital to Saint Francis Health System—an integrated health system with hospitals in Muskogee, Vinita, and Tulsa. William K. Warren Jr. says:

> I would like to be remembered as a team player. I think the wise counsel I was given was to surround myself with people who were smarter than me.... So, I think that I am a manager of people. I hope I've had this vision to see niches for the success of Saint Francis Health System. And I think you learn those niches by reading industry periodicals, coming up with ideas that you can test with people who are knowledgeable. So, I'd like to be remembered as a team player.

HENRY BELLMON

Twice Oklahoma's governor, US senator, education advocate—how would he like to be remembered?

> That question was asked of me at the end of my second term as governor. I'd like to be remembered as a governor who faced the issues squarely and dealt with them intelligently, and maybe courageously.

Afterword

While *Voices of Oklahoma* has recorded many stories for our website, we are unable to record all the important stories in our state. Stories such as yours that are very important to your family. And so, we encourage you to record your family story.

You may have heard the stories of your loved ones down through the years, but having their voices recorded will be embraced by future generations.

Years ago, recording an interview with a relative required a tape recorder and reel-to-reel or cassette tapes. But now, thanks to modern technology, you can record interviews and oral histories at a moment's notice on handheld devices. To aid you in this endeavor, you can search for "oral history questions" on your computer, or consult many recording apps.

You will be glad you recorded their stories. It is a wonderful way to preserve and respect the lives of your loved ones.

As a final note, I recorded my father's voice and story years ago and it is a pleasure to hear him speaking today. It keeps his memory close.

— *John Erling*

John Erling

AUTHOR BIOGRAPHY

Following his retirement from his top-rated morning radio talk show on Tulsa's KRMG, John Erling hardly rested on his laurels (which included induction into the Oklahoma Broadcasters Hall of Fame). After a three-year sojourn in advertising, he turned his attention to two of his first interests: Oklahoma history, and how oral history could contribute to Oklahoma history. The result, in 2009, was the founding by Erling of *VoicesofOklahoma.com*, a website (and now a podcast) that includes more than 200 interviews with Oklahomans from all walks of life—from statesmen (and women) to entertainers, and from sports heroes to unsung heroes of World War II. The success of *VoicesofOklahoma.com* is demonstrated by its continued growth, its wide acceptance by both teachers and students, and Erling's induction into the Oklahoma Historians Hall of Fame.

John Hamill

AUTHOR BIOGRAPHY

Author, journalist, and public relations practitioner, John Hamill has served in nearly every aspect of the communications industry. From newspaper, radio, and television, to editor of *TulsaPeople* magazine. From a congressional press secretary to spokesperson for Tulsa Public Schools. Beginning with the *Tulsa Spirit* book in the 1970s, Hamill has contributed to, authored, or coauthored six books on Tulsa and Oklahoma history. This is his seventh.

Index